Resilient Leadership for Turbulent Times

A Guide to Thriving in the Face of Adversity

Jerry L. Patterson, George A. Goens, and Diane E. Reed

Published in partnership with the
American Association of School Administrators

ROWMAN & LITTLEFIELD EDUCATION

A division of

ROWMAN & LITTLEFIELD PUBLISHERS, INC.
Lanham • New York • Toronto • Plymouth, UK

Published in partnership with the American Association of School Administrators

Published by Rowman & Littlefield Education
A division of Rowman & Littlefield Publishers, Inc.
A wholly owned subsidiary of The Rowman & Littlefield Publishing Group, Inc.
4501 Forbes Boulevard, Suite 200, Lanham, Maryland 20706
http://www.rowmaneducation.com

Estover Road
Plymouth PL6 7PY
United Kingdom

British Library Cataloguing in Publication Information Available

Library of Congress Cataloging-in-Publication Data

Patterson, Jerry L., 1944–
   Resilient leadership for turbulent times : a guide to thriving in the face of adversity / Jerry L. Patterson, George A. Goens, and Diane E. Reed.
      p. cm.
   Includes bibliographical references.
   ISBN 978-1-60709-533-0 (cloth : alk. paper) — ISBN 978-1-60709-534-7 (pbk. : alk. paper) — ISBN 978-1-60709-535-4 (electronic)
   1. School management and organization.   2. Educational leadership.   3. Resilience (Personality trait)
   I. Goens, George A.   II. Reed, Diane E.   III. Title.
   LB2805.P33813 2009
   371.2—dc22   2009028671

Printed in the United States of America

∞ ™ The paper used in this publication meets the minimum requirements of American National Standard for Information Sciences—Permanence of Paper for Printed Library Materials, ANSI/NISO Z39.48-1992.

Dedication

Jerry Patterson:
To my grandchildren, Alex, Jamal, Karim, and Lucy—you
enrich my life in so many ways. With deepest gratitude.
                                                    —Grandpa

George Goens:
To my grandchildren, Claire, Luke, Julia, and Caleb—
moments with you are golden.
                                                 —Grandpa G.

To Marilyn for bringing my whistle back.
                                                     —George

Diane Reed:
To my son, Bradley, and my daughter, Ashley—thank you
for teaching me more about life than I could ever teach
you.
                                                  —Love, Mom

Contents

Index to Figures and Tables

Part I

The Big Picture

Chapter 1

A Profile of Resilient Leadership

When President Hoover announced on the eve of the Great Depression that prosperity for America is "just around the corner," he was broadly criticized as blindly optimistic, not in touch with the severity of the times. When President Carter declared that a "national malaise" was the central culprit behind our economic downtown in the 1970s, he was accused of being too pessimistic, not offering any vision of hope.

In the early months of his presidency, Barak Obama offered a different perspective. With what universally was considered the worst set of circumstances facing a U.S. president since the Great Depression, President Obama tried to strike a balance that escaped Hoover and Carter. In his first speech to a joint session of Congress, President Obama declared his belief in the resilience of the American spirit and the American will. "We will rebuild, we will recover, and the United States will emerge stronger than before." President Obama did not minimize the severity of our crisis, punctuated by a banking system in total disarray, a stock market trapped in a downward spiral of gloom, and a housing market collapse that sent shock waves through the economy. At the same time, the President refused to concede his hope for the future.

President Obama saw the country as resilient, not only recovering from adversity but growing stronger in the process. The President moved swiftly from talk to actions during his first 100 days of service. Even though the impact of these actions awaits future judgment, Obama modeled several strengths of resilient leaders that we discuss in this book.

Our work with educational leaders across the nation has led us to a similar conclusion. Even in the toughest of times, educational leaders consistently demonstrate the ability to recover, learn from, and developmentally mature when confronted by chronic or crisis adversity. This definition of resilient leadership rests on a solid foundation of research-based principles and strategies to support leaders as they struggle to successfully overcome adversity.

In this book we draw upon the resilience research and best practices to answer the *how* question, "How can leaders move ahead in the face of adversity?" We define leaders broadly to include those who occupy positions of formal authority and those who informally lead others because of their expertise, credibility, and relationships. This book will benefit leaders who have confronted adversity in the past, struggle with adversity right now, or will likely encounter setbacks in the future. In each chapter we present current research and lessons we learned from interviewing more than twenty educational leaders. Our goal is to help leaders not only survive but thrive in the face of adversity.

In this chapter we begin the discussion with a description of the resilience cycle, an overview of the three critical skill sets necessary to strengthen leader resilience, and in the final section we invite leaders to complete the Leader Resilience Profile (LRP) at the end of the chapter. This information will be applied in subsequent chapters. After each resilience strength is discussed, leaders can analyze their relative resilience in this area as measured by the LRP.

LOWS AND HIGHS OF RESILIENCE

Resilience is not an all-or-nothing, fixed characteristic. Resilience is a relative concept. So even though we use the term *resilient leaders* throughout the book, we really mean leaders who are *relatively* more resilient than others. Resilience is also cyclical. In this section we discuss five phases of the resilience cycle, and we apply real-life examples of school leaders as they describe how they navigated these phases.

The cycle, illustrated in Figure 1.1, begins with the phase called *normal conditions*. Imagine a leader moving forward on cruise control. Things are going well in the organization. Teacher morale is high, resources are plentiful, and the community offers a lot of support to the system. Ray Denton, an assistant superintendent in a highly regarded Tennessee school district, experienced these conditions for several years, and as he put it, "Life was good."

Then adversity struck when a certain school board member and ambitious city council officials formed a coalition around an agenda to fire his mentor and respected superintendent. Denton told us in an interview, "This was someone personally very close to me, a personal friend as well as a mentor. He had been a leader for over ten years during my career as teacher, assistant principal, and central office administrator."

The Resilience Cycle

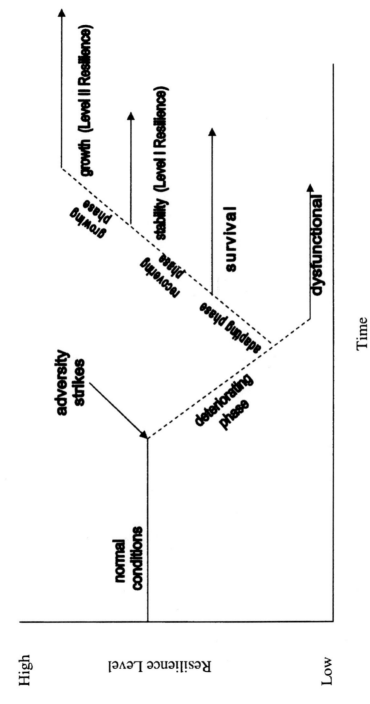

Figure 1.1. The resilience cycle

When the political winds strongly shifted in the direction of firing the superintendent, Denton and others in the district quickly slid down a slippery slope into phase two, the *deteriorating phase* of the resilience cycle. Pearsall (2003) described the deteriorating phase this way: "we react like kindling wood being added to fire. At least for a while, we think in ways that cause our problems to heat up and become more intense. We become angry and even aggressive. We blame others or degrade ourselves. We become our own and our problems' worst enemy" (Pearsall, pp. 8, 9). The emotions of denial, grief, and anger thrust leaders into the victim role for a period of time.

Denton observed that he was stuck in a very unhealthy phase. He felt like a victim of politics. He was disillusioned. He tried to hide both physically and emotionally. "When people asked me how I was doing I would say that the tallest blade of grass is the first to get cut by the lawnmower so I was doing my best not to get noticed." The stress also spilled over into his personal life. As he recounted, "My children were in the district, so when you are worried about what's happening in the school system as a whole and your own children are there, you have a much higher stake in the outcome. It affected my physical and emotional health. I gained weight and generally had more problems than I had ever had before." Denton saw himself as a victim of circumstances.

Phase two, the *adapting* phase, begins when leaders finally start to assume some responsibility for their condition and stop wallowing in the mire as victims. When asked what caused him to make the shift, Denton reflected and then said he finally came to terms with the fact that this was not the way to live his life and the way to perform his work. Another wake-up call was sounded by his physician, who told Denton he needed to lose 50 pounds, particularly since he had recently been diagnosed as diabetic, a familiar diagnosis in his family history. Finally he decided he had to personally engage and take some action to avoid staying stuck at the dysfunctional level of the resilience cycle.

The first thing he did to move to the *adapting phase* was to wake up to the reality that he had been very politically naïve about what was going on right in front of his eyes. "I think that I wore it as a badge of honor that we didn't do 'politics' in our district. We didn't let politics enter into our decisions." But he said he lost his innocence in a hurry. And it helped to have been studying in a doctoral leadership course about the political frame of leadership. He learned that the political frame is a reality, not necessarily an evil force designed to punish those on the other end of the force. "There was a skill gap that I needed to work on. It gave me something concrete to do." The second thing Denton did is assume personal responsibility to get his weight under control. He conceded that he was not in the clear yet, but had made a start in the right direction.

Continuing an upward trajectory, the adapting phase gives way to the *recovering phase,* a path back to the level of stability experienced before the onset of adversity. We refer to this status quo point as Level I resilience. Denton discussed concrete strategies he applied to help him recover. He began to listen more in situations that helped him understand the nature of power. He came to terms with the reality that power struggles exist in his shattered illusion of a district filled with harmony. Denton elaborated, "We either use it (the reality) or we deny it. I don't have to like it, but I better understand it, because I saw what happened to someone I cared about because he didn't have this tool in the toolbox." Eventually, the superintendent was fired, but he continues to live in the community, and Denton remains in his district leadership role.

If leaders plateau at the status quo level, they may continue to function adequately but they don't experience growth from the many lessons learned from adversity. Truly resilient leaders don't settle for the status quo. They enter the *growing phase* on their way to strengthened resilience. Pearsall (2003) called this the thriving level, "We thrive when we surpass and transcend our prior level of functioning, regain and even accelerate our upward psychological trajectory, and seem to have mentally and emotionally benefited from our suffering. Because of our crisis, we seem to begin to flourish. Thrivers aren't masochists who seek or somehow endure pain better than others, but they do tend to be rational optimists who learn from it, know when to fight or flow with it, and when to give in and move on." (pp. 17, 18).

We observed in our conversations with Denton that he appeared to have recovered and was moving into the *growing phase* of becoming even stronger. We asked him specifically what he learned and how he has grown. "I've learned to work with the board and not be afraid of them. They represent the politics of what we do. They are the visible presence of the politics that has to adhere to a system where lots and lots of money is being spent doing something that is very important to a community." Another thing Denton learned upon reflection is that he had been a rather isolated leader in the past. This led to a very limited network of relationships with other leaders. "I needed to build that. So now, for example, I have lunch with a couple of principals every now and then. This is also part of appreciating and nurturing the political frame to ensure that you know what is happening to the people around you." Denton said he felt such knowledge of political reality is part of making their job easier and will, he expects, make his job easier.

Finally Denton said that he has grown and become more optimistic in several ways. He works hard to find and maintain a sense of humor in tough times. As one illustration, "I Googled 'motivator websites' and discovered several rich sources." He even takes the motivational sayings and turns them around in a "Dilbert sort of way." He added, "It is a way to laugh at yourself, to laugh at the little games that we play in these group situations. It would even come up sometimes on my computer during meetings and say things such as: Leaders are like eagles . . . we don't have any of those around here."

We asked Assistant Superintendent Denton if he had any closing thoughts on lessons learned that would help others grow in the face of adversity. He paused, reflected a few moments and then offered these suggestions, "Number one, don't forget the politics. Number two, you're either going to be a light or you're going to shut light out. I'd rather be a light. It doesn't always mean cracking a joke. It means someone who is going to be brightness for others. At times this may mean I need to lean on somebody else who's brighter than me that day, but there's got to be somebody holding the torch."

It was clear during the interviews that Denton did indeed move in a healthy way through the phases of the resilience cycle, and he will be a torchbearer for others in their struggles with adversity.

THREE SKILL SETS OF RESILIENT LEADERS

In the previous section, we described the resilience cycle all leaders move through after they encounter serious adverse circumstances. The cycle concludes with Level II resilience. At this level, resilient leaders *demonstrate the ability to recover, learn from, and developmentally mature when confronted by chronic or crisis adversity.* Author Warren Bennis said that resilience is at the center of successful leadership. "I believe adaptive capacity or resilience is the single most important quality in a leader, or anyone else for that matter, who hopes to lead a healthy meaningful life."

We identified through our work with educational leaders three broad skill sets that are required of a resilient leader: resilience *thinking skills, capacity skills,* and *action skills.* In this section, we present an overview of the three skill sets. In Chapters 2–10, we examine each skill set in detail, carefully describing the concepts and action strategies to strengthen the skill. In addition, we provide specific *how to* examples from the ranks of leaders at all levels who have successfully demonstrated resilience skills.

Resilience Thinking Skills

The road to leader resilience starts with the skill set of thinking. When adversity occurs, many times leaders don't have a say about the nature or intensity of adversity facing them. But they do have a choice in how they think about the conditions they face. This interpretation filter consists of two components. First, how do leaders make sense of the reality of the present? Resilient leaders want to understand, as accurately and clearly as possible, both the bad news and the good news. They want to hear from diverse and even dissident voices so they can act from a comprehensive picture of reality.

In addition to understanding reality, how do leaders interpret future possibilities? Resilient leaders demonstrate an optimistic view about what's possible. They strive to make something positive out of a negative situation, and they maintain high expectations that something good can come from the adverse circumstances confronting them. In summary resilient leaders demonstrate the ability to have a positive outlook about the future in the face of adversity. At the same time, they don't deny the constraints posed by reality. We call this realistic optimism and we discuss the concept more in Chapter 2.

Resilience Capacity Building Skills

Large or small, chronic or crisis, adversity is virtually inevitable. How leaders choose to respond, however, is optional. This choice is determined in part by the skill set of resilience capacity. Think of resilience capacity as the fuel tank that supplies necessary energy to produce resilient actions. The amount of fuel in the tank is what leaders depend on to get them through rough waters to safe harbor. At a given point in time, the boundaries of resilience capacity are somewhat defined by a leader's accumulated experiences. The good news is that resilience capacity is elastic over time. As leaders get stronger by successfully confronting adversity, they expand their fuel tank and, by definition, their capacity to successfully weather future storms.

Four fuel sources comprise the resilience capacity of leaders: personal values, personal efficacy, personal well-being, and personal support base.

A leader's personal values structure consists of three levels. Perched in the top tier are a leader's ethical values, the moral compass that guides a leader's life work. As we discuss in more detail in Chapter 3, ethics is what defines a leader's character. Ethical values should never be situational. They transcend time and context. Next in the hierarchy are the educational values that bring a leader joy, meaning, and fulfillment in the job. In "Joy and Resilience: Strange Bedfellows," (Patterson, Goens, & Reed, 2008), we argued that educational values are about what matters most to leaders as they make tough choices among competing values and self-interest pressure groups. The third level within the personal values structure comprises the core values specific to program initiatives in the organization. Examples at this level include: What are a leader's core values about reading instruction, continuous student assessment, and expectations for success by *all* students? Program values drive the actions a leader expects in the classroom or district.

Personal efficacy, another critical source of resilience capacity, is demonstrated by a leader's confidence and competence to do the right thing when confronted by adversity. A resilient leader with a grounded sense of personal efficacy:

- Has confidence in his or her ability to reason, make decisions, and assume responsibility for personal actions when confronted with high stakes situations.
- Helps others develop a sense of efficacy in doing their work and meeting obligations.
- Adheres to core principles and values in making decisions. The leader does not sell out, just doing what's easy or expedient.
- Develops a track record of leadership competence in serving others.

A strong sense of personal efficacy relates directly to positive personal well-being, a third major energy source in resilient leaders. This energy source consists of three ingredients: physical well-being, emotional well-being, and spiritual well-being. As we interviewed leaders about their resilience capacity, they were quick to point out that, among all the resilience strengths, they struggle most to sustain personal well-being when the going gets rough. As accumulated setbacks start to take a toll, leaders who fail to renew and replenish these precious resources become less resilient and less immune to protecting themselves when facing turbulence in the future.

The fourth source of resilience capacity is the leader's ability to tap into a network of caring and support. Within the compartments in the capacity fuel tank, personal support ranked highest in leaders commenting on what they need to regain confidence in difficult times. In our interview, we found four common threads that appear essential for a strong support base: support of family, friends, colleagues, and mentors. We elaborate on each of these in Chapter 5.

Resilience Action Skills

This skill set is the litmus test of a leader's ability to recover, learn from, and developmentally mature in the face of adversity. A leader can demonstrate satisfactory resilience thinking skills in the form of a realistic appraisal about what's happening now and what is possible in the future. The leader can draw from an ample capacity of personal values, personal efficacy, personal well-being, and personal support. But if the leader does not *act* on the courage of convictions, especially during difficult times, then everything else is just talk.

Resilience action skills happen when the leader models the well-worn cliché, "Walk your talk." Specifically, our research pointed to four areas of resilient action. Resilient leaders show *perseverance* when they stay true to the course already set, refusing to let adversity prevail. When life inevitably disrupts even the best-laid plans, the resilient leader demonstrates *adaptability* by resisting the temptation to retrench to the old ways of handling things. An adaptable leader seeks flexible and creative approaches to get through the tough times. *Courage* under fire is evident when a leader takes principled action, even when some things about the situation are still ambiguous or confusing. Finally, a resilient leader takes *personal responsibility* for mistakes and corrective action in those situations where he or she contributed to the adversity in the first place.

SUMMARY

Our extensive research and review of best practices led us to identify three skill sets of resilient leaders and nine resilience strengths. The relationship between the major skill sets and the individual resilience strengths is shown in Figure 1.2. In the balance of the book, we devote a separate chapter to a discussion of each of the strengths and the accompanying action strategies to build on these strengths.

LEADER RESILIENCE PROFILE

After our research team identified these resilience strengths, we next asked the question, "How can leaders measure their relative resilience strengths?" The answer was a short one. Not very easily. While we were able to locate a handful of leader resilience instruments, such as the *Adversity Quotient,* the *Resilience Quotient,* and the *Survival Profiler,* we concluded there needed to be a more comprehensive measure to better serve leaders in their quest to strengthen resilience.

So we set about the task of developing the Leader Resilience Profile (LRP)®. First our research team conducted an exhaustive review of the literature in the fields of leadership and resilience. The research led us to identify initially sixty-two indicators of resilience. We used the indicators to construct a Web-based survey designed to solicit feedback from a panel of experts regarding the extent to which the survey accurately measures

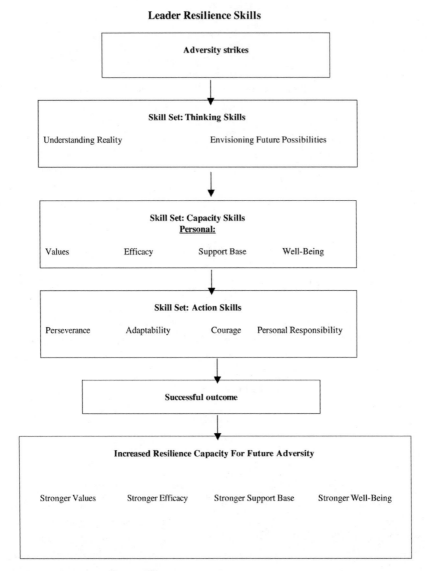

Figure 1.2. Leader resilience skills

what the research team intended on the subject of leader resilience. After we analyzed the data from the reviewers, we added, deleted, and modified items to strengthen the content validity of the LRP. Based on these revisions, we developed the "end user" instrument containing 73 items designed to measure leader resilience. A *Technical Supplement* (Patterson, Patterson, Reed, & Riddle, 2008) details the statistical results for measures of validity and reliability.

DETERMINE YOUR LEADER RESILIENCE STRENGTHS

Now it is time to personalize the research concepts we have outlined in this chapter. The first step is for you to complete the Leader Resilience Profile (LRP) below. If you prefer to complete the survey on line and instantly obtain your full profile, go to the link: www.theresilientleader.com

After you take the LRP survey, you then will use this information in subsequent chapters to assess your relative resilience on the strength we are examining in a given chapter. When you complete the book, you will also have completed a full profile analysis. By drawing on the concepts, experiences from other school leaders cited in this book, plus the action strategies that we highlight for each strength, you should be well on your way to thriving in the face of adversity.

LEADER RESILIENCE PROFILE SURVEY

The purpose of the Leadership Resilience Profile® (LRP) is to provide you an individualized profile of your resilience strengths. It will take you less than 30 minutes to complete the LRP. After you finish, you use this information in subsequent chapters to chart your profile for a specific strength.

Now that you have completed the LRP, let's continue the journey to stronger resilience. In Part Two, we will examine Leader Resilience *Thinking Skills,* comprising a comprehensive understanding of reality and an understanding of future possibilities. In Part Three, Leader Resilience *Capacity Skills,* we devote specific chapters to the skills of personal values, personal efficacy, personal well-being, and personal support base. Part Four is where the action is. We examine the Leader Resilience *Action Skills* of perseverance, adaptability, courageous decision making, and personal responsibility.

At the conclusion of the chapters on each skill set, you can chart your resilience strengths for the skill set we just examined. In this way, by the time you complete the book your overall, personalized profile will be available for you to assess your relative resilience strengths and apply the action strategies outlined in this book to help you be more resilient than ever.

Table 1.1. Leader Resilience Profile

Instructions: For each of the items, fill in the circle above the number that best describes where your leadership behavior fits on the continuum from being like the statement on the left to being like the statement on the right. "1" means your leadership behavior in the face of adversity is strongly reflected by the statement on the left. "6" means your leadership behavior is strongly reflected by the statement on the right. Marking numbers 2, 3, 4, or 5 reflects positions in between.

When Confronted With Adversity in My Leadership Role:

Item	Statement	My Leadership Behavior	Statement
1	I always have a positive influence in making things happen.	o o o o o o 1 2 3 4 5 6	I never have a positive influence in making things happen.
2	I don't have an overall sense of competence and confidence in my leadership role.	o o o o o o 1 2 3 4 5 6	I have an overall sense of competence and confidence in my leadership role.
3	I always use feedback about current reality plus what's possible in the future to make adjustments in my leadership strategies.	o o o o o o 1 2 3 4 5 6	I never use feedback about current reality plus what's possible in the future to make adjustments in my leadership strategies.
4	I never manage my time so I can achieve rest and recovery.	o o o o o o 1 2 3 4 5 6	I always manage my time so I can achieve rest and recovery.
5	I have a track record of being able to take appropriate action, even when some things about the situation remain ambiguous or confusing.	o o o o o o 1 2 3 4 5 6	I have a track record of not being able to take appropriate action, when anything about the situation continues to be ambiguous or confusing.
6	I never accept responsibility for making difficult leadership decisions that may negatively affect some individuals or groups.	o o o o o o 1 2 3 4 5 6	I always accept responsibility for making difficult leadership decisions that may negatively affect some individuals or groups.
7	I always try to prevent current adverse circumstances from happening again.	o o o o o o 1 2 3 4 5 6	I never try to prevent current adverse circumstances from happening again.
8	I never reach out to build trusting relationships with those who can provide support in tough times.	o o o o o o 1 2 3 4 5 6	I always reach out to build trusting relationships with those who can provide support in tough times.

#	Statement	Scale	Statement
9	I always adjust my expectations about what is possible based on what I've learned about the current situation.	○1 ○2 ○3 ○4 ○5 ○6	I never adjust my expectations about what is possible based on what I've learned about the current situation.
10	I don't demonstrate the overall strength of physical well-being needed to effectively carry out my leadership role.	○1 ○2 ○3 ○4 ○5 ○6	I demonstrate the overall strength of physical well-being needed to effectively carry out my leadership role.
11	I always take prompt, principled action on unexpected threats before they escalate out of control.	○1 ○2 ○3 ○4 ○5 ○6	When unexpected threats occur, I never take action before the threats escalate out of control.
12	When I choose to take no leadership action in the face of adversity, I never accept personal accountability for this choice.	○1 ○2 ○3 ○4 ○5 ○6	When I choose to take no leadership action in the face of adversity, I always accept personal accountability for this choice.
13	I always expect that good things can come out of an adverse situation.	○1 ○2 ○3 ○4 ○5 ○6	I never expect that good things can come out of an adverse situation.
14	When adversity strikes, I never try to learn from the experiences of others who faced similar circumstances.	○1 ○2 ○3 ○4 ○5 ○6	When adversity strikes, I always try to learn from the experiences of others who faced similar circumstances.
15	I always demonstrate the ability to put my mistakes in perspective and move beyond them.	○1 ○2 ○3 ○4 ○5 ○6	I never demonstrate the ability to put my mistakes in perspective and move beyond them.
16	I never draw strength during adversity from my connections to a higher purpose in life or causes greater than myself.	○1 ○2 ○3 ○4 ○5 ○6	I always draw strength during adversity from my connections to a higher purpose in life or causes greater than myself.
17	I always take prompt, decisive action in emergency situations that demand an immediate response.	○1 ○2 ○3 ○4 ○5 ○6	I never take prompt, decisive action in emergency situations that demand an immediate response.
18	I always have trouble accepting accountability for the long-term organizational impact of any tough leadership decisions I make.	○1 ○2 ○3 ○4 ○5 ○6	I always accept accountability for the long-term organizational impact of any tough leadership decisions I make.
19	I always pay attention to external forces that could limit what I would like to accomplish ideally.	○1 ○2 ○3 ○4 ○5 ○6	I never pay attention to external forces that could limit what I would like to accomplish ideally.

(Continued)

Table 1.1. (Continued)

Item	Statement	My Leadership Behavior	Statement
20	I always try to offset any relative weakness I have in an area by turning to others who have strength in this area.	○ ○ ○ ○ ○ ○ 1 2 3 4 5 6	I never try to offset any relative weakness I have in an area by turning to others who have strength in this area.
21	I never demonstrate an overall strength of adaptability in my leadership role.	○ ○ ○ ○ ○ ○ 1 2 3 4 5 6	I always demonstrate an overall strength of adaptability in my leadership role.
22	I always draw strength from my sense of spirituality in the face of adversity.	○ ○ ○ ○ ○ ○ 1 2 3 4 5 6	I never draw strength from my sense of spirituality in the face of adversity.
23	I never am able to make needed decisions if they run counter to respected advice by others.	○ ○ ○ ○ ○ ○ 1 2 3 4 5 6	I am always able to make needed decisions, even if they run counter to respected advice by others.
24	I demonstrate an overall strength of making courageous decisions in my leadership role.	○ ○ ○ ○ ○ ○ 1 2 3 4 5 6	I don't demonstrate an overall strength of making courageous decisions in my leadership role.
25	I don't have an overall strength of accepting personal responsibility for my leadership actions.	○ ○ ○ ○ ○ ○ 1 2 3 4 5 6	I have an overall strength of accepting personal responsibility for my leadership actions.
26	I always focus my energy on the opportunities to be found in a bad situation, without downplaying the importance of obstacles.	○ ○ ○ ○ ○ ○ 1 2 3 4 5 6	I always focus my energy on the obstacles, not the opportunities, found in a bad situation.
27	I never have a strong support base to help me through tough times in my leadership role.	○ ○ ○ ○ ○ ○ 1 2 3 4 5 6	I always have a strong support base to help me through tough times in my leadership role.
28	I can always emotionally accept those aspects of adversity that I can't influence in a positive way.	○ ○ ○ ○ ○ ○ 1 2 3 4 5 6	I can never seem to emotionally accept those aspects of adversity that I can't influence in a positive way.
29	During adversity, I never feel a deep sense of spiritual gratitude for the opportunity to pursue a calling of leadership.	○ ○ ○ ○ ○ ○ 1 2 3 4 5 6	During adversity, I always feel a deep sense of spiritual gratitude for the opportunity to pursue a calling of leadership.
30	I always make value-driven decisions even in the face of strong opposing forces.	○ ○ ○ ○ ○ ○ 1 2 3 4 5 6	I never make value-driven decisions even in the face of strong opposing forces.

#	Statement (left)	Scale	Statement (right)
31	I never gather the necessary information from reliable sources about what is really happening relative to the adversity.	1 2 3 4 5 6	I always gather the necessary information from reliable sources about what is really happening relative to the adversity.
32	I always maintain a respectful sense of humor in the face of adverse circumstances.	1 2 3 4 5 6	I am never able to maintain a sense of humor in the face of adverse circumstances.
33	I always let adversity in one aspect of my life have a long-term impact on the resilience in other parts of my life.	1 2 3 4 5 6	I never let adversity in one aspect of my life have a long-term impact on the resilience in other parts of my life.
34	When adversity strikes, I always avoid taking action until I've sufficiently gained control of my emotions.	1 2 3 4 5 6	When adversity strikes, I always take action before I've sufficiently gained control of my emotions.
35	I never protect sufficient time and space for renewing the spirit.	1 2 3 4 5 6	I always protect sufficient time and space for renewing the spirit.
36	I always demonstrate the overall strength of being a resilient leader.	1 2 3 4 5 6	I never demonstrate the overall strength of being a resilient leader.
37	I never demonstrate an overall strength of optimism in my leadership role.	1 2 3 4 5 6	I always demonstrate an overall strength of optimism in my leadership role.
38	I persistently refuse to give up in overcoming adversity, unless it's absolutely clear all realistic strategies have been exhausted.	1 2 3 4 5 6	I stubbornly refuse to give up in overcoming adversity, even when it's absolutely clear all realistic strategies have been exhausted.
39	I never emotionally let go of a goal that I commit to, even at the expense of sacrificing goals and values that are more important to me.	1 2 3 4 5 6	I always emotionally let go of a goal that I am pursuing, if it's causing me to sacrifice goals and values that are more important to me.
40	I possess an overall strength of spiritual well-being in my leadership role.	1 2 3 4 5 6	I don't possess the overall strength of spiritual well-being in my leadership role.
41	I never seem to look for the positive aspects of adversity to balance the negative aspects.	1 2 3 4 5 6	I always try to find the positive aspects of adversity to balance the negative aspects.
42	I always seek perspectives that differ significantly from mine, when I need to make tough decisions.	1 2 3 4 5 6	I never seek perspectives that differ significantly from mine, when I need to make tough decisions.

(Continued)

Table 1.1. (Continued)

Item	Statement	My Leadership Behavior	Statement
43	I never try to find new or creative strategies to achieve positive results in a difficult situation.	1 2 3 4 5 6	I always search for various new or creative strategies to achieve positive results in a difficult situation.
44	During adversity, I always sustain a steady, concentrated focus on the most important priorities until I achieve successful results.	1 2 3 4 5 6	During adversity, I never sustain until success is reached a steady, concentrated focus on the most important priorities.
45	I never demonstrate an understanding of my emotions during adversity and how these emotions affect my leadership performance.	1 2 3 4 5 6	I always demonstrate an understanding of my emotions during adversity and how these emotions affect my leadership performance.
46	I always rely on strongly-held moral or ethical principles to guide me through adversity.	1 2 3 4 5 6	I never turn to moral or ethical principles to guide me through adversity.
47	I never seem to accept the reality that adversity is both inevitable and many times occurs unexpectedly.	1 2 3 4 5 6	I always accept the reality that adversity is both inevitable and many times occurs unexpectedly.
48	I am always confident that I can learn something from my adversity to help me be stronger in the future.	1 2 3 4 5 6	I am never confident that I can learn something from my adversity to help me be stronger in the future.
49	I always let disruptive forces and other distractions interfere with my focus on important goals and tasks.	1 2 3 4 5 6	I never let disruptive forces and other distractions interfere with my focus on important goals and tasks.
50	I always create time for replenishing emotional energy.	1 2 3 4 5 6	I never create time for replenishing emotional energy.
51	I never seem to be able to privately clarify or publicly articulate my core values.	1 2 3 4 5 6	I am always able to privately clarify or publicly articulate my core values.
52	I always accept the reality that adversity can disrupt my best-laid plans or current projects.	1 2 3 4 5 6	I never accept the reality that adversity can disrupt my best-laid plans or current projects.
53	I never take a deliberate, step-by-step approach to overcome adversity.	1 2 3 4 5 6	I always take a deliberate, step-by-step approach to overcome adversity.

#	Left statement	Scale	Right statement
54	I always demonstrate an overall strength of perseverance in my leadership role.	○ 1 2 3 4 5 6 ○	I never demonstrate an overall strength of perseverance in my leadership role.
55	I never have the overall strength of emotional well-being in my leadership role.	○ 1 2 3 4 5 6 ○	I always have the overall strength of emotional well-being in my leadership role.
56	I always take leadership actions consistent with what matters most among competing values.	○ 1 2 3 4 5 6 ○	I never base my leadership actions on what matters most among competing values.
57	I don't possess the overall strength of understanding current reality in my leadership role.	○ 1 2 3 4 5 6 ○	I am proud of demonstrating an overall strength of understanding current reality in my leadership role.
58	I always demonstrate the essential knowledge and skills to lead in tough times.	○ 1 2 3 4 5 6 ○	I never demonstrate the essential knowledge and skills to lead in tough times.
59	I never seem to find healthy ways for channeling my physical energy to relieve stress.	○ 1 2 3 4 5 6 ○	I always find healthy ways for channeling my physical energy to relieve stress.
60	I never let adverse circumstances that inevitably happen disrupt my long-term focus on maintaining a healthy lifestyle.	○ 1 2 3 4 5 6 ○	I always let adverse circumstances that inevitably happen disrupt my long-term focus on maintaining a healthy lifestyle.
61	I never seek feedback to see if my leadership actions are matching my values.	○ 1 2 3 4 5 6 ○	I always seek feedback to see if my leadership actions are matching my values.
62	I always accept responsibility for making needed changes personally in those cases where I contributed to the adversity.	○ 1 2 3 4 5 6 ○	I never seem to accept responsibility for making needed changes personally in those cases where I contributed to the adversity.
63	I never maintain a confident presence as a leader in the midst of adversity.	○ 1 2 3 4 5 6 ○	I always maintain a confident presence as a leader in the midst of adversity.
64	I always quickly change course, as needed, to adapt to rapidly changing circumstances.	○ 1 2 3 4 5 6 ○	I never quickly change course, as needed, to adapt to rapidly changing circumstances.
65	I never monitor my personal health factors, then adjust my behavior accordingly.	○ 1 2 3 4 5 6 ○	I always monitor my personal health factors, then adjust my behavior accordingly.
66	I always demonstrate an overall strength of being value-driven in my leadership role.	○ 1 2 3 4 5 6 ○	I never demonstrate an overall strength of being value-driven in my leadership role.

(Continued)

Table 1.1. (Continued)

Item	Statement	My Leadership Behavior	Statement
67	I never seem to acknowledge my mistakes in judgment as a leader.	○ ○ ○ ○ ○ ○ 1 2 3 4 5 6	When I make mistakes in judgment as a leader, I publicly accept responsibility to avoid making these mistakes in the future.
68	I never hesitate to tell those I trust about my doubts or fears related to adversity.	○ ○ ○ ○ ○ ○ 1 2 3 4 5 6	I never tell those I trust about any of my doubts or fears related to adversity.
69	I am always determined to be more persevering than before when confronted with the next round of adversity.	○ ○ ○ ○ ○ ○ 1 2 3 4 5 6	I never seem determined to be more persevering than before when confronted with the next round of adversity.
70	I never try to learn from role models who have a strong track record of demonstrating resilience.	○ ○ ○ ○ ○ ○ 1 2 3 4 5 6	I always actively seek to learn from role models who have a strong track record of demonstrating resilience.
71	I always seek the most current, research-based information about how to sustain healthy living in stressful times.	○ ○ ○ ○ ○ ○ 1 2 3 4 5 6	I never seek the most current, research-based information about how to sustain healthy living in stressful times.
72	I never turn to personal reflection or introspection to steady myself during adversity.	○ ○ ○ ○ ○ ○ 1 2 3 4 5 6	I always turn to personal reflection or introspection to steady myself during adversity.
73	I am always comfortable sharing with my support base any small wins I achieve along the road to recovering from adversity.	○ ○ ○ ○ ○ ○ 1 2 3 4 5 6	I am never comfortable sharing with my support base any small wins I achieve along the road to recovering from adversity.

Part II

Resilience Thinking Skills

Chapter 2

Understanding Reality and Envisioning the Future

Stories from school leaders across the United States confirm that the bumper sticker is right: *Shift happens.* And many times the shift is *bad shift* that demands a quick reaction by leaders. So they react and then something else happens because of their reaction. This sets in motion a chain reaction that feels to leaders like they are playing a game of organizational bumper cars, being hit from every direction and struggling to get in a few licks of their own.

It's tough to remain optimistic under these conditions. But it's possible! In this chapter we describe how it is not only possible but very likely to happen as leaders strengthen their resilience thinking skills. First we examine the concept of realistic optimism. What is it, and why is it important in leadership roles? Next we outline action strategies that focus on present reality as well as future possibilities. How can leaders make sense of their current reality, and how can they make a difference in the future, even during the most difficult times?

WHAT IS OPTIMISM?

Let's start with what optimism is not. Optimism as a psychological concept is not a short-term phenomenon. With all of the challenges leaders face in their leadership role, understandably they have days when they are discouraged about the future and other days that offer them plenty of reasons for encouragement about what lies ahead. Even though these fluctuations reflect temporary changes in mood or disposition, they aren't a barometer of overall optimism. As Paul Houston, former Executive Director of the American Association of School Administrators, explained, "If leaders adopt a short-term view of optimism, things are going to happen that aren't good. These leaders go from day to day on the roller coaster ride from the high of optimism to the sudden downward spiral toward pessimism. There is no stability to rely on." A long-term view of the future, according to Houston, "makes it almost impossible not to be resilient, because this too shall pass. And I will have a lot of other shots at this before it is over." Building on Houston's perspective, our emphasis related to resilience thinking skills is on how leaders *generally* imagine prospects for the future, keeping in mind that they will encounter setbacks and speed bumps along the way.

Also, optimism about the future is not the same as a forecast about whether certain future events will happen. For instance, a school administrator may declare she is very optimistic that the economic and fiscal conditions of the school district will improve in eighteen months. In reality, she is simply forecasting or projecting the future stability of the district based on current assumptions. She has little or no control over the political or economic forces at play in the state or nation. Her forecast can be positive or negative, but control is not in her hands. However, she has direct influence over where the school district places its budget priorities and spending. This is an intended future outcome she can influence.

Now let's turn to what optimism *is* within the context of leadership. Optimism is a long term phenomenon reflecting how leaders generally perceive the world from their viewpoint. Specifically, *an optimistic leader maintains a positive outlook about the future in the face of adversity, without denying the constraints posed by reality.*

We refer to this as *realistic* optimism. In earlier research Patterson and Kelleher (2005) found that optimism is a relative term ranging from extreme pessimism to unbridled optimism. The authors identified four profiles of leaders on the pessimism-optimism continuum shown in Table 2.1.

We define, in summary form, each of the profiles:

- *Unrealistic pessimists* have a pervasive, rather permanent interpretation of adversity that happens to them, and they have no confidence that anything positive will come out of the adversity.
- *Realistic pessimists* have a reasonably accurate interpretation of reality, but they hold a bleak view of the future and don't think their efforts will make much of a difference.
- *Unrealistic optimists* are quick to make judgments about reality without taking the necessary time to digest what is truly happening. They underestimate the risks that adversity poses, and they firmly believe that they can make their highest hopes become reality in the future, despite the severity of adversity they face.

Table 2.1. Pessimism-Optimism Continuum

Category	Unrealistic Pessimists	Realistic Pessimists	Realistic Optimists	Unrealistic Optimists
Understanding Reality				
Assumptions about reality	Deny that the assumptions are true	Acknowledge that the assumptions are true, magnify their negative impact, and see them as barriers	Acknowledge that the assumptions are true and refuse to accept them as barriers	Dismiss the assumptions as insignificant to progress
Causes of current reality	Find other people and forces totally at fault	Accept some responsibility, but primary cause is others	Accept responsibility for their contribution to the current reality	Assume they know the causes, but don't invest the time to accurately assess reality
Risks posed by current reality	Greatly overestimate the risks caused by adversity	Understand the risks and place undue weight on the negative	Accurately assess the risks by striving to have enough data to judge	Discount the risks and refuse to see how they may jeopardize the future
Envisioning Future Possibilities				
Ability to influence future	Refuse to see how they can make any difference	Believe any difference they may possibly make won't be worth the personal effort	Believe strongly they can positively influence the future, within certain constraints	Assume they will, without a doubt, have a major influence on the future
Expectations for future success	Can't see any possibility for a positive future	Hold low expectations that anything good will happen	Believe good things may happen, but it will require a lot of work	Assume the best-case outcomes will happen
Focus of future efforts	Focus exclusively on worst-case outcomes	Heavily emphasize the negative side of the problem	Acknowledge problems, but choose to emphasize the positive possibilities	Focus only on perfect solutions

- *Realistic optimists* seek to understand fully what is really going on, including how they may have played a role in causing the adversity. They also
  believe they can make a difference in the future, despite the pressures posed
  by reality.

In summary, the way leaders think about current reality and future possibilities shapes how they tackle crisis or chronic adversity. We recommend realistic optimism as the most effective world view of choice for resilient leaders.

WHY IS OPTIMISM IMPORTANT?

The short answer is that researchers have documented evidence that a person's level of optimism makes a profound difference in the quality of their
lives. Some of the more recent findings include:

- Optimistic individuals have better social relationships as well as higher levels of physical health, academic and athletic performance, recovery from
  illness and trauma, pain tolerance, self-efficacy, and flexibility in thinking
  (Cameron, Dutton, & Quinn, 2003, p. 53).
- Optimists see adversity as a challenge, transform problems into opportunities, persevere in finding solutions to difficult problems, maintain confidence, rebound quickly after setbacks, and persist (Schulman, 1999, p. 32).
- Optimists are easily motivated to work harder, are more satisfied and have
  higher morale, have high levels of motivational aspiration and stretch goals,
  persevere in the face of obstacles and difficulties, analyze personal setbacks
  as temporary, and tend to feel upbeat and invigorated both physically and
  emotionally (Luthans, 2002).

In addition to these findings about the importance of optimism, other
researchers have documented that these resilience strengths can be learned
by children as well as adults. Reivich and Shatte (2002) described a proven
program to demonstrate how resilience can be strengthened.

In the balance of the chapter, we discuss action strategies that realistic
optimists apply to help them *maintain a positive outlook about the future in
the face of adversity, without denying the constraints posed by reality.*

ACTION STRATEGIES TO STRENGTHEN OPTIMISM

When adversity strikes, resilient leaders realize they cannot move ahead
effectively without an accurate picture of what is truly going on amid the
adversity. They view their situation through the lens of a realistic optimist.

Our research found that realistic optimists relentlessly implement the following strategies to help them make sense of their world.

Action Strategy: Resilient Leaders come to Terms with the Reality that Adversity Likely will Show up Unexpectedly and Disrupt their Best-Laid Plans

It is understandable that leaders feel the pressure and the responsibility to prevail and move ahead in the face of adversity. Those they serve look to leaders as a shield from the multiple attacks trying to disrupt the organization's plans for the future. Also leaders' personal resilience is boosted if they spend their resilience energy on making good things happen as planned. What happens in reality, though, is that even though considerable energy is spent trying to keep disruptions at bay, they keep popping up unexpectedly. These surprise visits have a tendency to wreak havoc in the organization and drain the personal resilience of leaders.

Many leaders move through these seemingly endless bouts with adversity mumbling "if only" pleas. If only the state department would leave us alone, we could get the job done. If only we didn't have unplanned surprises that block our progress, we could be in fine shape.

The *if only* pleas are a natural reaction to adversity. And it's natural for all leaders to wish that adversity would evaporate and leave them and their organization alone. When wishes don't come true, realistic optimists learn to think about reality differently than their more pessimistic colleagues.

Realistic optimists avoid being repeatedly surprised at the unexpected detours set up by outside forces. They engage in strategic thinking, examining current reality and anticipating possible actions and futures. In this way, they prepare themselves mentally to expect the unexpected. As one school leader told us, "I have found that it doesn't truly drain my resilience when I'm surprised. It drains my resilience when I'm surprised I'm surprised. So I have to come to terms with the fact that unexpected stuff is going to happen. I also have to let go of the belief that I can wish away the adversity. This change in thinking frees me up to spend my energy concentrating on how I can make sense of the adversity in a meaningful way."

Another school leader, a Midwestern superintendent, gave this account after a tough night at the table with the school board.

"When I finally got home about 2 a.m. looking rather pitiful, my wife asked what went wrong this time? I said, 'I was caught off-guard by the board's actions. The board had given me assurance they were going to support the administration's recommendations for rezoning schools. Then when we get to the vote, they registered a 5–2 vote against the recommendations. I know what happened. They listened to the politically connected residents who spoke at the meeting, and then they caved in. It just caught me off guard, I guess."

"My wife smiled as she reminded me, 'Didn't you tell me about a month ago they did a flip-flop on what you expected related to support for the computer initiative, and didn't you tell me that it was because a bunch of loud community voices intimidated them?' I reflected on her comments and then grudgingly acknowledged, 'Yeah, you're right. So what you're telling me is that I shouldn't have been surprised tonight by the unexpected. But what could I have done differently?'"

Optimistic leaders realistically expect that unexpected disruptions can happen to best-laid plans and so they prepare themselves and their staff accordingly. In response to the question the superintendent posed to his wife, he could have convened a meeting with his immediate staff in advance of the board session to have a conversation such as the following:

"Don't be surprised if the board flip-flops tonight on what they said they were going to do about the rezoning. It will become a political process and we can't control it. What we can do is: first, prepare ourselves for the possibility. Second, we need to schedule a meeting now to occur within the next two days in case we have to go back to the drawing board to make sense out of the new reality they could manufacture for us tonight. If that happens, we have to figure out how to make lemonade out of lemons . . . again."

It's important to note that the superintendent wasn't behaving as a pessimistic leader when he prepared his staff for a possible surprise. He didn't act like the victim and blame the perpetrators of the crime. He didn't forecast it was definitely going to happen. What he did is act in a way that conveyed the strong message, "We refuse to drain our resilience by being surprised by a shift in reality, and we refuse to roll over and play victim. We are going to regroup and figure out how to make sense of whatever happens so we can move ahead in a way that is best for this community."

Action Strategy: Resilient Leaders Gather all Relevant Information, from as many Credible Sources as Possible, about what is Really Happening

When adversity strikes and disrupts the status quo, realistic optimists launch a multifront attack to learn what is actually occurring. They look in all corners and crevices to uncover and discover the most objective analysis possible about reality. It means taking the risk to seek diverse perspectives about what is going on, including perspectives that radically depart from their own assessment of reality. It means taking all steps necessary to seek out the bad news. As one assistant superintendent said to her staff, "When we find ourselves in a mess around here, I want to know everything. The good, the bad, and the ugly. And let's start with the bad and ugly. Don't hide it from me." The bad and ugly side of reality is important to help realistic optimists have as much solid data as possible in order to know how to make sense of it and what to do about it. Realistic optimists reduce the probability of future surprises by knowing in advance what lies beneath the heavy rocks of adversity.

Seeking diverse perspectives about the reality of the situation means that leaders expose themselves to the likelihood that credible sources will interpret reality differently than the leaders. And this in turn means that leaders may need to reassess their own interpretation. Even though it is more energy draining in the short run to contend with bad news and divergent perspectives about reality, in the long run there is positive payback.

Unrealistic optimists take the shortcut of denying the bad news or discounting its importance. They send messages that they don't want to hear perspectives that reject or question their own analysis. They don't have time for the dissonance it creates. In the long run, though, they pay the price for their short-sightedness when their misdiagnosis of reality causes long term pain as they now have to spend their scarce energy on damage control. In the long run, denying or discounting reality drains, rather than conserves, leader resilience.

In his role as superintendent in Wisconsin, Jerry Patterson hired an administrator from a neighboring district as the assistant superintendent of business services. "I remember telling Don," Patterson said, "that he had a track record for speaking his mind, and that he wasn't shy about disagreeing with the superintendent on occasion. I told him I wanted to build a culture that was open to diverse perspectives, even if it meant challenging my views."

Don quickly lived up to this reputation. "There were times," Patterson recalled, "that I wanted to send him back to where he came from. We would be moving ahead on an issue with a united front, and then he would counter with a perspective that I had not and did not want to consider."

More often than not, however, the diverse perspectives helped Patterson and the district have a more comprehensive sense of what truly was happening when crisis occurred, politically or educationally.

Action Strategy: Resilient Leaders Pay Attention to the Reality of any External Forces that could Limit what they would like to Accomplish, Ideally

Among the many strategies we identify in this book to build resilience for leaders, we get the most resistance from leaders on the need for this strategy. They argue that resilient leaders should believe that nothing will be allowed to get in the way of their efforts to overcome adversity. This belief is, indeed, inspiring in the short run. The research is very clear, however, that failure to recognize the nonnegotiable upper limits of what can be accomplished drains leadership resilience in the long run, because leaders spend precious energy attempting to overcome obstacles that their reality check tells them are insurmountable. For example, significant and sustained budget cuts imposed on an organization do have limiting effects on what leaders wish they could accomplish. To pretend otherwise is to engage in self-deception that takes a long-term toll on leaders and those they are leading. Realistic optimists can still demonstrate their resilience by dreaming big about what can be accomplished within the financial constraints they must work within.

So, as we show repeatedly throughout this book, we believe in optimism, even optimism that borders on illusion. At the same time we have no evidence that long-term resilience is strengthened by delusionary dreams of what is possible. Consider the following scenario as an illustration.

A newly hired urban superintendent addressed the opening-day assembly of 2,000 staff members. She was fired with passion as she said to the audience, "I pledged to the school board during the interview process that, if I'm appointed to this position, we will be known within twelve months as a world-class school district. Well, here I am today as your new superintendent, and I want to reiterate what I told the board. We will do whatever it takes to become a world class-school district this year and I will accept nothing less."

The staff that the superintendent addressed came to the meeting with a realistic history of the district, one apparently not possessed by the superintendent. For ten years, student enrollment had decreased an average of 1,000 students per year. Due in part to student exodus and, in part, to poor financial conditions of the state, budgets had been slashed repeatedly, some of the most talented teachers had abandoned the district for more attractive jobs, and morale was at an all-time low. Staff members were hungry for hope and for someone who believed in them, but they knew that there was no way they could deliver on the superintendent's expectations for them.

A year later at the annual town hall meeting, the school board asked the superintendent to report on her pledge to produce a world-class school district. The district had made progress during the year, but by no stretch of the imagination could the superintendent claim a world-class school district. In her report the superintendent leveled criticism at the staff for not delivering on expectations, and her remarks were broadly covered in the media. Morale dipped lower and six months later, the superintendent quit the district in the same condition as when she came into the district, fired with passion.

We began Chapter 1 of this book with reference to remarks made by President Obama in his first address to the joint session of Congress. We indicated that the President conveyed to the American people that his belief in the resilience of this nation is tempered by his realization that progress will not come easily. In his words, "I suffer no illusions that this will be an easy process. Once again, it will be hard." And during his first months in office, the President continually reminded the nation of the outer limits of what can be expected in the short run. We contend that resilient leaders suffer no delusions that overcoming adversity will be an easy process. Similar to President Obama, though, resilient leaders believe they can recover, rebuild, and become stronger than ever in the long run.

Action Strategy: Resilient Leaders Search for the Positive Aspects of the Adversity to Balance the Negative Aspects

Realistic optimists take a comprehensive approach to developing a clear picture of reality. They want to know, objectively, what is happening. On the other hand, realistic optimists take considerable latitude in how they choose to construe the adversity that is happening to them. They shift their thinking orientation from objective to subjective as they search for positive meaning in negative situations. Again, we are not lobbying for subjectivity that goes beyond the boundaries of what reasonable leaders should conclude. We are lobbying for the position that even the worst news has positive aspects. We realize the natural response to adversity is to assume the role of victim or, as Seligman (1991) described the condition, learned helplessness. Individuals habitually react rather mindlessly under crisis conditions.

Realistic optimists take a more mindful, active approach by deliberately *reframing* the situation. They actively search for the positive side that offsets the negative side. Realistic optimists approach adversity by asking, "What are the truthful, positive elements contained in the mess we face?" In difficult and even painful times, opportunities present themselves.

A positive interpretation of a bad situation can include giving others the benefit of the doubt regarding their motives for causing the adverse circumstances. Understandably school leaders tend to lay blame at the feet of the superintendent who surprises the principals with an announcement that most principals will be reassigned to different schools. If, however, principals can legitimately find favorable probable cause that motivated the superintendent to decide that reassigning principals is a good thing to do, it frees up principals to focus their resilience energy positively on how they can make the future work for, not against, them.

Another example of reframing is to shift the emphasis from a focus on the problems to a focus on the challenges that reality presents. We don't mean a cosmetic recasting of language. We mean an authentic shift from spending resilience answering the question, "What are all of the problems within the reality we face now?" to "What challenges does this predicament pose for us?" Most leaders feel empowered by a challenge to overcome but feel drained by a long list of apparently insurmountable problems.

Reframing the meaning of reality to search for the positive side also helps leaders find some appreciation for the lighter side of a generally dark adversity. An elementary principal in the Southwest said he has been reporting to the same central office administrator for the past ten years. The principal said, "I annually expected and received a very high score on my end-of-year performance evaluation. But the superintendent retired this past June and now I am confronted with a new reality. My new supervisor just met with me to discuss my performance and I received what I regard as quite negative marks in two categories. I get the feeling that I am not very appreciated around here anymore."

The principal can interpret the evaluation in a way that concludes "the superintendent doesn't appreciate me" or the principal can reframe reality by asking "what can I find to appreciate about the negative marks?" Perhaps, for example, the principal had become accustomed over time to rather mindlessly moving through the year without reflecting on his performance. The negative marks this year may cause him to reflect on the areas that have been allowed to drift in recent years. The realistic optimist may be relieved to have the blind spot called to his attention, so he can better align his commitment to excellent performance with a renewed demonstration of excellent performance.

The above strategies focus on how to strengthen leader resilience by accurately and thoroughly assessing the state of affairs related to adversity that happens. The second component of resilience thinking skills is *envisioning future possibilities*. Referring again to Figure 1.2 in Chapter 1, even though conducting an objective analysis of the reality is a necessary skill for resilient thinking, it is not sufficient. Resilient leaders also need to demonstrate their skills in maintaining a positive outlook about the future in the face of adversity, without denying the constraints posed by reality. In this section we examine concrete strategies to strengthen the thinking skills that shape the future.

Action Strategy: Resilient Leaders find ways to have a Positive Influence in Making Good Things Happen

"The Little Engine That Could" famously captured the spirit of a *can do* attitude when he exclaimed between huffs and puffs on his uphill climb, "I think I can, I think I can." Resilient leaders capture this same spirit. They believe they can make a positive difference when the uphill climb looks forbidding. It all starts with a belief in *self.* Resilient leaders have a strong sense of efficacy. They demonstrate confidence and competence that they can influence the future in a positive way. In Chapter 4 we expand on this concept, but for now we want to emphasize that resilient actions aimed at making a positive difference depend on positive thinking and feeling. The rapidly growing field called positive psychology focuses on assets of the leader, not the liabilities.

Leaders have considerable latitude in how they choose to respond to adversity. Recall from our earlier discussion that their choice is not simply a stimulus-response interaction, but is framed by how they think about what they can do. Resilient leaders demonstrate resilient thinking skills by responding to adversity with *how can I* thinking. How can I make a positive difference? Notice the contrasting impact on resilience when the same adversity is approached, instead, with *if only* thinking. "If only I didn't face this uphill battle, then I could maybe make a difference." We are reminded once again that optimistic leaders think differently from pessimistic leaders. And this difference is in how they choose their response to the adversity.

We asked Drake Sinclair, a veteran school district superintendent in Minnesota, about how he applied "how can I" thinking when his district faced radical annual budget reductions for about seven years. Sinclair offered this perspective, "You're right that the cuts were radical, and I asked myself the question, 'How do I give people optimism and hope at a time when we are cutting lots of teachers and good programs?'" Sinclair answered his own question by saying that he believed in himself. He knew he could make a difference. He said he needed to be in the forefront showing that his actions matched his beliefs. "I spent a great deal of my time cheerleading, trying to have people in the face of adversity always look for ways to improve their programs. I think that people would say that we maintained a sense of optimistic leadership and that we continued to talk about the good things we did as a district instead of how awful things were. From my point of view, that really buoyed our schools. We had people coming up with magnificent changes in their programs. That was the real focus of our leadership group."

Drake Sinclair consistently referred to "we the leaders" in his remarks about making a positive difference. Sinclair was being modest because it was crystal clear to us in our discussions that he was the cheerleading leader who set the tone for the leadership team and, in turn, for the rest of the district.

Action Strategy: Resilient Leaders Strive to Prevent Current Adverse Circumstances from Happening Again

One of the common themes we discovered in our work with leaders across the world is the emphasis on life-long learning. Learning comes easily for leaders when the bumps on the road are few and far between. But when the going becomes a rough ride, understandably it is difficult for leaders to focus on the question, "What am I learning from all of this mess?"

Resilient leaders cultivate a *habit* of a learning orientation. In other words, they don't have to summons a lot of conscious energy to keep them focused on learning in the midst of crisis. Barbara Kelso, an associate superintendent in a progressive school district in the Northeast, echoed our belief in forming habits before a crisis strikes. "It goes back to before you ever encounter adversity. It's the habits and lifestyles that you have already developed. I don't think when you are in the midst of it all you can suddenly develop new relationships, new eating habits, and new workout habits." In other words, resilient leaders conserve their scarce energy in tough times by relying on an "automatic," practiced pattern of how to think about responding.

A second habit resilient leaders cultivate is the habit of reflection. They don't necessarily engage in heavy-duty reflection when they are in the thick of adversity. They save their reflective energy for the period after the storm when they can capitalize on the advantage of time removed from the negative circumstances to reflect on what they learned. Less resilient leaders who do carve out time for reflection tend to frame their thinking with questions such as, "What did I do wrong? If I had it to do all over again, what would I do differently to keep bad things from happening?" This approach is manifest in pessimistic leaders who place the emphasis on repair, instead of growth.

Leaders who think like realistic optimists use their resilience thinking skills to reframe the questions. They ask questions like, "What did I learn from this situation that will help me reduce the chances that similar circumstances will occur again? How can I improve in the way that I approached adversity this time, without abandoning the things I did well?"

Several leaders we interviewed identified a common adversity they unsuccessfully tackled the first time around: failed school district referendums. The leaders talked about how they reflected and learned from the defeat so they could better position the organization for success the next time around. Sandra Jenkins, a nationally acclaimed superintendent in the Midwest, offered a story that paralleled other referendum stories of her colleagues.

Jenkins and the school board put forth a school district referendum that, in their collective wisdom, met the needs of the students and the community. School officials gathered significant data to justify the needs and to warrant the major expenditures supported by the referendum. Jenkins and other district leaders were confident that they knew what was best. The referendum was soundly defeated.

After licking their wounds for a while, the school district leaders decided to go forth again with a second referendum. But this time they decided to use a strategy they ignored the first time. They decided to ask the community what they needed and would support. Jenkins commented to us with a tinge of embarrassment, "You might wonder why we didn't do that in the first place. We wondered that, too." So in version two of the referendum process, district leaders held numerous listening sessions with various groups. "We were out there 50 nights during that next year. This also turned out to be a relationship building point in school community relations." Jenkins added, "I think we rose in their estimation of us. They knew we cared about what they had to say and wanted to serve them in the way they wanted to be served." Not surprisingly the second referendum passed. Lessons learned, according to Jenkins, were, "It was a communication lesson for us and a trust building experience for the community." In summary, the approach taken by Jenkins and colleagues during the second referendum is a vivid example of this resilience strategy in action. Resilient leaders strive to prevent current adverse circumstances from happening again.

Action Strategy: Resilient Leaders Expect Good Things will come out of an Adverse Situation

The key ingredient in this strategy is *positive expectations,* a fundamentally different way of thinking than positive wishing and hoping. Less optimistic leaders engage in wishful thinking that produces statements like "I sure wish that something good will come out of this." Realistic optimists think differently in response to adversity. Their thought processes lead them to say, "I expect that good things will happen." They are not at the mercy of the external forces in shaping the outcomes of adversity. Optimistic leaders hold high expectations in large part because they believe they can indeed influence the outcomes in a productive way and they act accordingly. They embrace the slogan, "Where there is a will there is a way." Not surprisingly, realistic optimists are strong-willed leaders who put high expectations on themselves and the organization to deliver positive outcomes in negative circumstances.

Even though resilient leaders hold high expectations, they are not perfectionists. Unrealistic optimists don't just hold high expectations for success. They hold unrealistically high expectations for perfection. Anything less is failure. While that is motivating in the short run, this way of thinking depletes the resilience energy in the long run because, by definition, perfection is rarely possible within the dynamics of the politics, complexity, emotions, and resource limitations leaders confront in the real world. Realistic optimists shoot for best-case outcomes and, if they miss the bulls-eye, they don't consider it a failure if they come really close.

Action Strategy: Resilient Leaders Focus their Energy on the Opportunities, not the Obstacles, found in a Bad Situation

Inherent in any adverse situation is a pile of obstacles blocking the path to success. We discussed in the first section of this chapter that realistic optimists don't deny the obstacles. In fact they want to uncover the scope and depth of the obstacles buried out of sight. The distinguishing feature of this Action Strategy is that pessimists see the glass as half empty and focus on the obstacles that caused the condition. Consequently they exhaust their energy attacking the enemies of success. Optimistic leaders, on the other hand, acknowledge the harsh reality of the obstacles but they see the glass as half full and spend their energy searching for every possible opportunity to create positive outcomes. They discover in the process that the search itself can be fulfilling. As one researcher described it, "People are not happy because of what they do, but because of how they do it" (Csikszentmihalyi, 1990). Resilient leaders draw positive energy and satisfaction from looking for the positives in a negative context.

Timothy Johnston, retired high school principal demonstrated this philosophy when we talked with her about her strength of optimism. She observed, "There are three kinds of people in life: the ones who see the glass as half full, the ones who see it as half empty and the ones who have no glass at all. I know them all. I always see the glass as half full. It is my natural orientation and it shapes the way I see people in situations. Sometimes people see this as a little Pollyanish, but I have used this strength to get me through some tough times. Optimism is where I put my emotional and intellectual focus."

When we asked associate superintendent Barbara Kelso what has been her foundation and source of strength for optimism, she replied, "In large part it was the environment I grew up in, such as longtime family members who are still vibrant even in their 80s and 90s. They are my role models. I think the world is great and you only have one life to live. Make the most of it and see the glass as half full, not half empty. Life is too short to dwell on the negatives."

Action Strategy: Resilient Leaders Maintain a Respectful Sense of Humor in the Face of Adverse Circumstances

A respectful sense of humor is a fragile, delicate skill when applied in a time of adversity. Peterson and Seligman (2004) acknowledged that humor is something that is much more easily recognized than defined, but nevertheless they offered the following meaning of the concept within the context of adversity: "a composed and cheerful view on adversity that allows one to see its light side and thereby sustain a good mood" (p. 584). Optimistic leaders use humor to shine some light on a dark subject. Assistant Superintendent Denton addressed this in Chapter 1 when he commented about converting real life downers into Dilbert style uplifting cartoons.

There are several instruments developed to measure the concept of humor, including one scale designed to measure humor in the face of adversity. The *Coping Humor Scale* (CHS) was developed to measure the extent to which individuals report using humor to cope with stress. At the applied level, one school leader told us, "I never allow a gloomy situation to take away from my sense of humor." Another school administrator said she can usually find something to laugh or joke about even in trying situations. Researchers (Peterson & Seligman, 2004) have found that humor as a psychological strength becomes particularly important in times of adversity because "it helps to mitigate, suppress, interrupt, or even permanently replace negative impact." (p. 595).

Although humor is generally seen as healthy by leaders, they acknowledge it is difficult to find something funny in unfunny circumstances. Sometimes leaders just have to laugh at the absolute absurdity of the situation. As one school principal commented to us, "You wouldn't believe the policy the school board just put in place about dress codes. The strictness of the policy is beyond what any reasonable person would create. So I told the staff that all we can do is laugh about it and try to make the best of a ridiculous situation." In this case laughter might be the best medicine.

One word of caution on the use of humor to soften the impact of a crisis. When leaders seek relief through humor in the midst of tragedy, it may backfire when the point is lost on those who bear the brunt of the tragedy. Funny is in the eyes of the beholder. Leaders need to distinguish between their private use of humor that helps them through tough times and the public application of humor in those circumstances that unintentionally comes across as disrespectful to others. An elementary school principal in Arizona recently called a staff meeting to deliver bad budget news. The entire state of Arizona, and schools in particular, were directed to make deep cuts in personnel. After delivering the news, the principal attempted a bit of humor when he quipped, "But, hey, by trimming staff maybe we will learn how to become lean and mean." Lean and mean was not how the staff wanted to be seen.

SUMMARY

In this chapter, we reviewed the first skill set of resilient leaders: resilient thinking skills. The first component in this set reflects the importance for leaders to fully understanding reality, what's happening here and now in the middle of adversity. The second skill entails leaders envisioning the future, an optimistic future filled with possibilities that leaders can influence. We examined nine action strategies to help leaders strengthen their resilience thinking skills. Now we provide you the opportunity to chart your own resilience profile for the resilience strength, *optimism.* Below are the instructions and format to measure the two components of optimism: understanding reality and envisioning future possibilities. We will repeat this activity following a discussion of each of the remaining strengths in Chapters 3–10.

CHARTING YOUR RESILIENCE PROFILE FOR OPTIMISM

To chart your Leader Resilience Profile for *Optimism,* return to your completed LRP Survey in Chapter 1, then follow these steps:

- For each item number listed, circle your *actual* item response on the chart.
- Determine the *conversion* score for the item, located directly beneath the *actual* number you circled.
- Enter your conversion score in the box on the extreme right column of the chart.
- Sum the scores in the right column to determine your Resilience Strength Score for Optimism. **Note:** You will have two separate subscale scores for Optimism: *Understanding Reality* and *Envisioning Future Possibilities.*
- Observe your individualized score on the continuum from Moderately Low to Very High.

Table 2.2. Optimism Subscale

Strength: Understanding Reality

Item #	Item Response	Enter your Conversion Score for the Item
19	If your *actual* item response is: 1 2 3 4 5 6 Then your *conversion* score is: 6 5 4 3 2 1 **enter your conversion score in the box →**	
31	If your *actual* item response is: 1 2 3 4 5 6 Then your *conversion* score is: 1 2 3 4 5 6 **enter your conversion score in the box →**	
41	If your *actual* item response is: 1 2 3 4 5 6 Then your *conversion* score is: 1 2 3 4 5 6 **enter your conversion score in the box →**	
47	If your *actual* item response is: 1 2 3 4 5 6 Then your *conversion* score is: 1 2 3 4 5 6 **enter your conversion score in the box →**	
52	If your *actual* item response is: 1 2 3 4 5 6 Then your *conversion* score is: 6 5 4 3 2 1 **enter your conversion score in the box →**	
57	If your *actual* item response is: 1 2 3 4 5 6 Then your *conversion* score is: 1 2 3 4 5 6 **enter your conversion score in the box →**	
	Strength Score: Understanding of Reality →	

Strength Score Continuum for Understanding Reality

Resilience Level →	Moderately Low	Moderate	Moderately High	Very High
Score Range →	13–18	19–24	25–30	31–36

Table 2.2. Optimism Subscale

Strength: Envisioning Future Possibilities

Item #	Item Response	Enter your Conversion Score for the Item
1	If your *actual* item response is: 1 2 3 4 5 6 Then your *conversion* score is: 6 5 4 3 2 1 **enter your conversion score in the box →**	
7	If your *actual* item response is: 1 2 3 4 5 6 Then your *conversion* score is: 6 5 4 3 2 1 **enter your conversion score in the box →**	
13	If your *actual* item response is: 1 2 3 4 5 6 Then your *conversion* score is: 6 5 4 3 2 1 **enter your conversion score in the box →**	
26	If your *actual* item response is: 1 2 3 4 5 6 Then your *conversion* score is: 6 5 4 3 2 1 **enter your conversion score in the box →**	
32	If your *actual* item response is: 1 2 3 4 5 6 Then your *conversion* score is: 6 5 4 3 2 1 **enter your conversion score in the box →**	
37	If your *actual* item response is: 1 2 3 4 5 6 Then your *conversion* score is: 1 2 3 4 5 6 **enter your conversion score in the box →**	
	Strength Score: Envisioning Future Possibilities →	

Strength Score Continuum for Envisioning Future Possibilities

Resilience Level →	Moderately Low	Moderate	Moderately High	Very High
Score Range →	13–18	19–24	25–30	31–36

Part III

Resilience Capacity Building Skills

Chapter 3

The Value-Driven Leader

During a recent administrative retreat on data-driven decision making, one of the principals was asked if he supported the idea. He responded, "It depends."

When pressed about his response, he elaborated, "It depends on the year. When we are up for accreditation review, we make sure we comply with all of the checklist demands by the state department of education involving the use of student data in tracking their progress. So we are heavily involved in data-driven decision making. In other years, though, we tend to lapse back into the old way of doing business."

Whether the topic is data-driven decision making, differentiated instruction, or brain-based learning, most school leaders who attempt all of the newest, trendiest innovations end up without focus. In other words they become event-driven, bouncing from one innovational event to another.

This event-driven mentality drains the individual resilience capacity of those asked to embrace the newest slogans as well as the leaders struggling to stay current on the latest innovations. Even though staying focused on what matters most is always hard for school leaders, it is particularly a struggle to stay focused when leaders are bombarded by adversity. Focus, in large part, is achieved through the careful identification and articulation of core personal values, followed by leadership actions that align with the values. In this chapter we examine action strategies that guide leaders as they a) construct and articulate to others their personal values, and b) take leadership steps designed to align their actions with their professed values. Throughout the discussion we present the perspectives of educational leaders who stayed the course of acting on their convictions, even in the face of storms that hit them.

ACTION STRATEGIES TO STRENGTHEN
PERSONAL VALUES

Action Strategy: Resilient Leaders Privately Clarify and Publicly Articulate their Core Values

Just like the companion slogans of vision and mission, the proliferation of writing about values has diluted the true meaning to the point of *no* common meaning. Leaders give personalized meaning to the topic of values when they establish a clear understanding of core values that relate to building resilient organizations. They are philosophical statements that guide leaders' intentions, actions and outcomes of their actions. They form the basis for character. These values become the philosophical basis for clarifying *why* leaders do what they do.

Leaders in a school district may require students to enter and exit through certain doors at the school. They may require students to walk, not run, in the hallways. They may demand that students leave dangerous objects at home. Leaders require this behavior, not because they are event-driven, but because of something deeper the school cares about. Because the school district values creating a safe environment where all students can learn, they hold student expectations such as those outlined here. Similarly, effective school leaders create school improvement councils not because administrators and teachers need another set of meetings to attend but because they value creating forums for open discussion about how the school can be even better than it is already. Until leaders become clear in their own minds about what they value, it's virtually impossible for them to become clear to others about what matters most.

Personal Values Hierarchy

Constructing a personal values hierarchy is one way to sort on those values that are most central to defining what leaders stand for. The personal values hierarchy we propose for leaders, shown in Figure 3.1, consists of three levels:

- Core ethical and moral principles
- Core educational values
- Core values about specific programs and initiatives

Ethical principles are core values that express what leaders stand for about right and wrong. These values are nonnegotiable, and transcend the mission, vision, and values of any leader's organization. Fullan (2001) referred to this concept as moral purpose, the social responsibility to others and the environment. At a global level, an example of a document articulating a set of

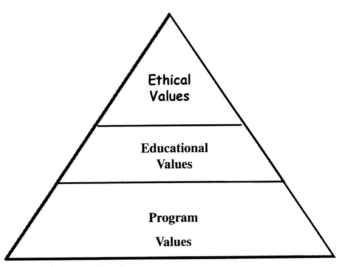

Figure 3.1. Personal values subscale

universal values about moral purpose is the United Nations' Universal Declaration of Human Rights. The declaration contains thirty articles intended to serve as a common standard for defining moral purpose for all peoples and nations. At a personal level, ethical principles held by leaders consist of themes such as "doing no harm," trustworthiness, responsibility, and caring.

A guide for personal ethical principles about right and wrong can be as simple as the belief in the Golden Rule or as complex as the doctrine of a religious faith. These values may also be anchored to a nondenominational spirituality that guides personal conduct. In all cases, ethical values tend to center on universal themes such as compassion, love, integrity, trust, and honesty. Examples of core ethical values are:

- I value acting in a trustworthy way.
- I value demonstrating compassion for all people.

When leaders run into the inevitable conflict between various values they hold, the deep-rooted core values about right and wrong take precedence in importance over other values the leaders hold.

School district administrator Barbara Kelso discussed her views about the role ethical values play in confronting adversity, "As leaders, you are likely faced with various challenges at different times and one's ability to successfully navigate those waters is really a part of who you are to begin with. It has to do with your passion, your beliefs, and your ethics as a core foundation." She added, "Sometimes going into turbulent waters you may not know they are turbulent until you get there." Roman also contended that these ethical principles are truly fundamental and that leaders must have strong passionate feelings about them.

Just as personal ethics guide the moral conduct of leaders, core educational values guide their overall educational practices. School districts in general, and schools in particular, exist to improve teaching and learning. Core educational values, therefore, center on what leaders value about excellence in teaching and learning. Sample core educational values include:

- I value organizing our organization's instructional strategies around the most current research and best practices.
- I value a school environment that holds *all* adults accountable for *all* students achieving at the highest level possible.
- I value a teaching and learning environment that emphasizes to everyone, "We believe in you, you can do it, and we won't give up on you."

Indeed, the school leaders we interviewed put students first in all matters. They didn't just talk about it. They did it!

The third level in the values hierarchy consists of program values that give meaning and direction to specific programs and initiatives in an organization. In the instructional arena, leaders need to able to publicly articulate answers to questions posed by staff and community such as, "What values do you hold that drive your leadership in our elementary reading program and our high school science program?" In the area of school district decision making, leaders need to clarify their values in significant areas like shared governance, consensus decision making, and the role of parents in school decisions.

Our intent in raising questions like these is not to imply there is one right answer to the questions. Our purpose is to amplify the importance that values play for leaders in giving meaning and direction to the program initiatives in their organization. To illustrate our point, consider the fact that a leading national educational organization recently advertised on their Web site the following professional development sessions offered by the organization:

- Closing the Achievement Gap
- Creating a Learning Community
- Developing Leadership Capacity
- Developing Literacy
- Differentiating Instruction
- Engaging and Motivating Students
- Planning Better Curriculum
- Supporting High-Quality Teaching

This is just a small slice of the range of programs offered by the organization.

As leaders contemplate which activities to choose in a tight fiscal environment, they are faced with difficult, trade-off choices about the most appropriate investment of scarce professional development funds. Unless leaders are clear about their *most important* program values, they have no solid basis to decide which "events" they undertake. A former Superintendent from Texas, Nathan England, commented in his visit with us, "There are four basic values that a leader has to provide a balance of: choice of freedom and liberty, equity and equality, responsibility to maintain a fiscally responsible operation, and excellence in teaching and learning. The problem is, these four values aren't mutually exclusive. If you pursue one of those values to exclusion of the others, then you diminish the others. Therefore the leader has a constant balancing act."

In our view, the balancing act is heavily influenced by a leader's values hierarchy. And as we argue throughout the book, ethics comes out on top.

Steps to Develop Personal Values

The previous section presented a conceptual framework for differentiating between various levels of personal values. In this section we describe some fundamental steps that will help leaders systematically approach the development of important personal values.

Step One: State the core value in a way that creates a clear image in the mind's eye. The core value process begins with a simple sentence describing what leaders care deeply about at a given level in the personal values hierarchy. This can be a statement about a core ethical principle such as trust, a core educational value such as student achievement, or a core program value like the topic of data-driven decision making. We want to underscore the importance of limiting a single value to a single philosophical statement that is absent jargon and is not merely a sweeping generalization such as, "I value educating every boy and girl to achieve his or her maximum potential in the 21st Century using technology." We are not suggesting the value is unimportant. We are adamant that any value must give clear, focused direction on how individuals and the organization should invest their scarce resilience energy.

To illustrate Step One, we use the ethical principle of being a value-driven leader:

Personal Value

- I value providing leadership anchored by a clear set of ethical principles that reflect what matters most to me and what others can expect from me.

By constructing core values about a leader's own personal values, the step creates a guide for how a leader will spend the currency in his or her resilience bank account. When leaders invest the time necessary to state in writing what they value, they push themselves to make clear what previously may have been fuzzy thinking in their own mind.

Step Two: Add the power of "I will" statements. To give added clarity and specificity to personal values, a second step is to add the power of *will* to the value statements. In this context, we are using the term *will* in two ways. We mean the will, or determination, to see the value come alive in daily practice. Without the will, value statements sit as idle commitments with no force of energy propelling the values into action. We also use the term to reflect what leaders will do to act on the value. Just as the *I value* statements are public disclosures of what leaders care most about, the *I will* statements are public declarations of what leaders expect of themselves and what others can expect from them related to the articulated value. Below are examples of *I will* statements applied to personal values.

Personal Value

- I value providing leadership anchored by a clear set of ethical principles that reflect what matters most to me and what others can expect from me.

  Therefore I will:

- Privately clarify and publicly articulate my core values
- Take leadership action consistent with what matters most among competing values
- Rely foremost on strongly held ethical principles to guide me through adversity
- Always make value-driven decisions even in the face of strong opposing forces
- Consistently gather feedback to make sure I am walking my talk

Step Three: Articulate personal values to others. After leaders construct their personal values about what matters most among competing values at the ethical, general educational, and program levels, they face a comparably challenging task to clearly and concisely articulate these values to those they are leading.

Imagine that a middle school faculty begins a new school year with a newly appointed principal. At the opening faculty meeting, the well-intentioned principal dims the lights, then begins the meeting with a PowerPoint presentation on his leadership values. His comments are laced together with phrases like strategic imperatives, systemic change, total quality improvement, and evidence-based performance by teachers. Succumbing to the dim lights and a principal who uses fuzzy slogans that don't appear remotely connected to student learning, faculty members' minds wander to more immediate things like, "What am I going to do the first day of school?"

With the best of intentions the principal engages in actions that produce unintended consequences. Faculty members, unclear on a vision the principal holds for the school, become skeptical that they may waste their resilience chasing slogans that don't lead anywhere. The principal, in turn, becomes frustrated with the faculty members and the needle on his own resilience tank heads toward the empty mark.

Action Strategy: Resilient Leaders Rely *Foremost* on Strongly Held Moral or Ethical Principles to Guide Them through Adversity

Some educational leaders will read this action strategy and understandably conclude, "I already do this. Next strategy, please." Leaders who are successful in the long haul have an established track record of ethical performance. So why spend time discussing ethical leadership? Our reply: leaders' ethical struggles aren't so much battles over right-versus-wrong. In fact, these are rather easy to reconcile. Do what's morally right. As most leaders will attest, the truly agonizing struggles occur over deciding right versus right. Most leaders experience angst, for instance, when they have to make tough budget cuts that affect certain programs disproportionately to others. It is not usually a matter of one program is good and another is bad. But a decision has to be made. We believe there are effective ways to approach thinking and acting in the most ethical manner possible. We outline below a framework for leading ethically.

Distinguish Between Ethical Principles and Other Important Principles

To aid in making the distinctions, we begin with what ethical leadership is *not*. Ethical leadership is not synonymous with:

- Following the law. A morally sound system of laws does not equate to ethical principles. Many laws that govern educational institutions pertain to policies and procedures that aren't ethical in intent. Also, there are laws on the record books in some countries that have the deliberate outcome of restricting the human rights of certain groups.
- Following religious doctrine. While most religions are based on moral principles, there are leaders who are not religious and yet act according to the highest ethical standards.

- Following culturally accepted norms. Even though we make take pride in living in a very ethical culture, slavery is a blatant example where we were culturally blind to moral, ethical principles about life, liberty, dignity, and respect for all individuals.

If ethical leadership is not the same as the above concepts, what is it? Ethicists, scholars, and religious leaders may debate the more academic versions of ethics, but we choose to focus on applied ethical leadership. Ethical leaders consistently live their lives in a way that is guided by principles of morality and virtue. More specifically, ethical leadership in action involves a leader's ethical values, principles, decisions, and actions aligned with the values. We make the following distinction between values and principles. Values are a leader's beliefs about what is morally right and virtuous. For example, "I value treating all people with dignity and respect." An ethical principle is basically converting a statement about what a leader believes to be important to what a leader (or any other individual) should do related to the value. "I *should* treat each person with dignity and respect." In other words the ethical principle becomes the standard by which to judge corresponding decisions and actions.

Distinguish Between Conditional and Unconditional Ethical Principles

The inability to make this distinction causes leaders to deplete their resilience capacity as they grapple without clear guidelines on how to decide between right and right. Unconditional ethical principles are reserved for those moral principles that should be followed without exception. For example, an unconditional ethical principle in an educational organization may state, "*All* people we serve, students, employees, and community members, should be treated with dignity and respect." No conditions attached.

Conditional ethical principles are those that meet the litmus test of *ethical* principles and, at the same time, should *not* be followed if they violate a higher order, unconditional ethical principle. For instance, a leader may operate from the following ethical principle, "All students are entitled to the right of freedom of expression unless it infringes on the basic human rights of others." Leaders who are clear on their unconditional ethical principles are also clear on actions they should take when confronted by competing values in the hierarchy.

To summarize, leaders foremost need to be clear about what constitutes their ethical values. Next, they need to be able to distinguish, first in their own mind and then to others, between what comprises their unconditional and conditional ethical principles. When this is accomplished, leaders are better able to preserve their resilience as they apply the next strategy of acting on these principles.

Action Strategy: Resilient Leaders Act on what Matters most to them among Competing Values

After leaders take the necessary steps to develop and articulate their core values, they must find the determination, or will, to make it happen. For many leaders, the will is demonstrated by taking the risky step to publicly declare, "This is what you can expect from me." Once said, leadership integrity is on the line regarding follow-through with promised actions. If leadership conduct does not align with leadership promises, leaders can rightfully be criticized for not "walking the talk."

Central to sustained leader resilience is establishing a pattern of alignment among three sets of dynamics shown in Figure 3.2, The Personal Strengths Triangle:

- What leaders say they value in relation to what they actually value (Say > Value)
- What they say they do in relation to what they actually do (Say >Do)
- What they actually do in relation to what they actually value (Do >Value)

The three anchor points of the Personal Strengths Triangle are Value, Say, Do. As we emphasized previously, *Value* refers to what leaders believe is

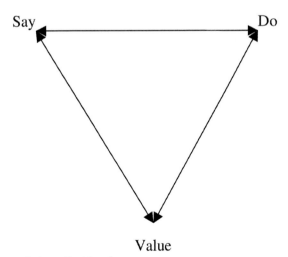

Figure 3.2. Personal strengths triangle

important. *Say* refers to what leaders talk about being important. *Do* refers to leadership actions connected to what they say is important. The relationship between what leaders say they value and what they actually value is a measure of their authenticity. Do leaders, on an ongoing basis, stand up for the values that they say are most important? The relationship between what leaders say they do and what they actually do is a measure of their reliability. Can leaders be counted on to follow through consistently in a dependable way by delivering on their commitments to action? The relationship between what they actually do and what they actually value is a measure of their character. How does a particular leader choose to live his or her life? Their patterns of actions, over an extended period of time, become outward symbols of their inner character. The Personal Strengths Triangle is like a mirror, reflecting to others the authenticity, dependability, and character of the leader.

Let's look at how the Personal Strengths Triangle applies in a real-life scenario. Barbara Kelso, the school administrator we interviewed in the Northeast, talked with us about a conflict the district administrators struggled with related to competing core values.

"There had been an employee issue regarding someone who had been directly insubordinate with the superintendent. After a careful investigation of his actions, the employee was terminated. The union, in conjunction with the newspapers, was pushing back on the decision because it had to do with freedom of speech. This value is obviously very near and dear to the media. So you have two extremely powerful organizations focusing on what was right and then you had the superintendent and board focusing on the value of the safety of students."

The issue escalated to the point that there was a serious death threat to the superintendent. In addition, publications within the statewide teachers' organization and the media publicly made derogatory comments about the administration. When asked what she learned from this experience, Kelso commented, "It was not so much new learning, but revisiting the point that when you take on issues that have very strong public implications, other people will certainly be ruthless and relentless in pursuit of their own values. But I have seen that as long as everyone knows how your leadership actions align with your values, they will have respect for that."

Amid the adversity created over the termination of an employee, district leaders were clear on what was most important to them in the battle of values between freedom of speech and student safety. And, according to Kelso, the district leaders acted in concert with the values that mattered most.

Another example of taking action consistent with what matters most among competing values was told to us by Lucinda Riaz, former superintendent in a small urban district in Florida. Riaz was confronted with the conflict of having to select between the conflicting ethical values of loyalty and integrity. Faced with serious budget shortfalls, the school board directed Superintendent Riaz to nonrenew all untenured teachers and bring a concrete plan for how she was going to do it. Riaz balked. In her words, "I had already been working on the problem with our human resources staff and the financial affairs officials at the state department. I was able to demonstrate that attrition would absorb the reductions we needed to make. Furthermore, if I carried out the Board's unnecessary directive, we would lose all of the new special education teachers plus math and science teachers we worked so hard to recruit. If we nonrenewed these teachers, they would be hired in a second by neighboring districts that were scrambling to secure talented teachers in these areas."

Superintendent Riaz examined these competing values she faced between having to decide between loyalty and integrity and she concluded, "I decided it was a moral value of mine in terms of what was best for the school system. So I told the Board, 'No, I won't do what you are demanding. I will not risk losing all of the employees we recently hired. We don't have to do that to balance the budget.' So I submitted my plan and the Board charged me with insubordination."

When we asked Riaz to elaborate on standing firm when it could put her job in jeopardy, she responded, "I chose to be insubordinate because I was not going to fire those teachers unnecessarily and adversely affect our students' quality of instruction. I am the one who has to get up in the morning and look in the mirror and ask myself if I did the ethical thing. And I did."

These real-life examples dramatically highlight what happens when two competing values vie for placement in the Personal Values Hierarchy. Sometimes, it even costs leaders their job. It did for Lucinda Riaz. But as we elaborate in Chapter 9, resilient leaders act on the courage of their convictions in spite of the adversity that confronts them.

Action Strategy: Resilient Leaders Consistently Gather Feedback to make Sure they are Walking their Talk

Resilient leaders want to know if their conduct matches their stated values, so they ask for periodic feedback about alignment among the three sets of dynamics reflected in the Personal Strengths Triangle. Many times a misalignment between leadership values and actions can be traced to what we call *behavioral drift*. That is, it is natural for leaders to develop patterns of behavior that have a tendency to drift away from what they truly care about. Particularly in times of adversity, leaders are under pressure to deliver on a number of fronts, and their values, efficacy, and energy are tested by the pressure. They may spend more time at the office than they intended. They may fall into the trap of skipping lunch to meet all of the demands on their schedule. It's unfair to characterize temporary behavioral drift as a sign of weakness, or a serious departure from stated values.

To help avoid any long-term patterns of behavioral drift, leaders can develop their own personal "virus shield" to detect misalignment between the three sets of dynamics in the Personal Strengths Triangle. For instance, leaders can create feedback mechanisms where colleagues or family members regularly provide candid comments about "walking your talk." They can issue a standing invitation for people to let them know when drift happens. Leaders show a sign of strength, not weakness, when they acknowledge that some-times they will make mistakes and engage in conduct that they didn't intend. By asking for immediate, direct feedback when drift occurs and then taking the necessary steps to bring actions, words, and values into better alignment, leaders become stronger, ready to take on bigger battles in the future.

By checking for alignment on a periodic basis, leaders can detect patterns of drift at the early stages before they become entrenched negative habits that are harder to correct. Also by taking early action on the behavioral drift, leaders spend their resilience currency on building strength rather than trying to repair a growing weakness.

Action Strategy: Resilient Leaders Make Value-Driven Decisions even in the Face of Strong Opposition

This action strategy could easily be converted to a headline banner on all job postings for school leaders: "Wanted: School leaders who will make value-driven decisions in the face of strong opposition." Opposition takes many forms, ranging from deeply held spiritual differences to highly charged political opposition. In some cases, district leaders face a very divisive community when they have to redraw attendance boundaries to serve a new high school. The political opposition can be vicious, with each constituency wanting to be certain neighborhoods with high caliber sports heroes remain in their attendance area. In other cases, opposing forces are aligned by ideology, arguing for banning certain books in the library or removing specific content from the district curriculum. In all cases, the expectation for leaders is the same. Resilient leaders should not succumb to the pressures of opposing forces.

Jerry Patterson authored a book, *The Anguish of Leadership* (2000), that told the story of the superintendency through the eyes of men and women who lived it. In the book, Patterson recounted the advice offered by a veteran superintendent to rookie leaders, "The advice is simple, watch out for rocks in your pocket. If you are doing your job right, eventually you will start accumulating rocks in your pocket from alienating certain groups of individuals because you can't please all of the people all of the time." And a recent *Pickles* cartoon strip carried the advice even further, "When you start collecting rocks in your pocket, make sure you wear a belt."

Leaders at all levels feel the cumulative weight of rocks in their pocket as they make principled decisions in the face of opposition. Sometimes the opposition stems from leaders having to take urgent, emergency action. There isn't time for consensus building. On other occasions, leaders act in opposition to advice by supervisors and peers. We described earlier the opposition by the school board that Lucinda Riaz confronted. There is also the constant pressure by single-agenda groups for leaders to take actions that satisfy their interests. Regardless of the source of the opposition, leaders can't go wrong when they anchor their actions in deeply held principles.

SUMMARY

Among the strongest of strengths identified by resilient leaders is their passion to be value-driven in all they do. Their moral compass is calibrated on what matters most to the leaders, ethically, professionally, and programmatically. In this chapter we provided a format for leaders to consider in helping them privately clarify and public articulate their values as well as strategies to make the values come alive in practice. We also outlined steps that leaders can take to check for behavioral drift, a condition that affects everyone. Finally we illustrated the principles we discussed through real-life stories of resilient leaders who are value-driven. This resilience strength is the central foundation on which all other strengths depend.

CHARTING YOUR RESILIENCE PROFILE
FOR PERSONAL VALUES

To chart your Leader Resilience Profile for *Personal Values,* return to your completed LRP Survey in Chapter 1, then follow these steps:

- For each item number listed, circle your *actual* item response on the chart.
- Determine the *conversion* score for the item, located directly beneath the *actual* number you circled.
- Enter your conversion score in the box on the extreme left of the chart.
- Sum the scores in the left column to determine your Resilience Strength Score for *Personal Values.*
- Observe your individualized score on the continuum from Moderately Low to Very High.

Table 3.1. Personal Values Subscale

Strength: Personal Values

Item #	Item Response	Enter your Conversion Score for the Item
30	If your *actual* item response is: 1 2 3 4 5 6 Then your *conversion* score is: 6 5 4 3 2 1 **enter your conversion score in the box →**	
51	If your *actual* item response is: 1 2 3 4 5 6 Then your *conversion* score is: 1 2 3 4 5 6 **enter your conversion score in the box →**	
56	If your *actual* item response is: 1 2 3 4 5 6 Then your *conversion* score is: 6 5 4 3 2 1 **enter your conversion score in the box →**	
61	If your *actual* item response is: 1 2 3 4 5 6 Then your *conversion* score is: 1 2 3 4 5 6 **enter your conversion score in the box →**	
46	If your *actual* item response is: 1 2 3 4 5 6 Then your *conversion* score is: 6 5 4 3 2 1 **enter your conversion score in the box →**	
66	If your *actual* item response is: 1 2 3 4 5 6 Then your *conversion* score is: 6 5 4 3 2 1 **enter your conversion score in the box →**	
	Strength Score: Personal Values →	

Strength Score Continuum for Personal Values

Resilience Level →	Moderately Low	Moderate	Moderately High	Very High

Chapter 4

Efficacy and Resilient Leadership

Men make history, and not the other way around. In periods where there is no leadership, society stands still. Progress occurs when courageous, skillful leaders seize the opportunity to change things for the better.

—Harry S Truman

Jack played with his salad, moving pieces of lettuce from one corner of his plate to the other. "I don't know, June, maybe I'm not cut out for this job, anymore."

She looked at him and said, "Come on, Jack, you're so accustomed to being successful all the time that one fly in the ointment has thrown you for a loop."

"Yeah, but it's a big loop. I don't know if I have it any more. That experience cost me big time with my board members, and threw a load of doubt as to whether or not I can make a difference anymore."

"Sooner or later, Jack Rinko, we all experience something like this . . . we crash," June said. "You'll bounce back. Don't forget the contributions you've already made to the district. You know you can learn from failures too, probably more than from your successes."

"Maybe. But it never occurred to me that I could blow it like this. It has caused me to wonder whether I'm in the right place and job."

"The district really needs you," June said emphatically, looking straight into Jack's eyes. "They look to you in good times and bad times, Jack. If you wilt, they will too."

Jack's conversation with June over lunch raises issues that all leaders face at one time or another. Crises happen, dilemmas bubble up and confusion occurs. And yes, mistakes are made. All of these create stress and pressure.

OVERVIEW OF LEADER EFFICACY

Leadership has two dimensions: the internal and external. In Jack's case, he is suffering internally, questioning several things: his ability to continue to contribute, whether he is in the right position, and whether he's meeting expectations. His internal angst, in this case, is caused by external pressure and the interface of his abilities and performance with the complexity and challenges in the larger context.

June raises a key issue. She sees the impact on Jack, but she also suggests it affects the district too. The external world—the schools, community, and others—looks to leaders in tough times. They require confident leaders who, despite some missteps in the past, can help them move forward to face challenges. They need leaders they can believe in.

Winston Churchill is a prime example of a leader who failed, but in times of severe challenge and distress, the British turned to him because of his sense of efficacy, purpose, and presence. He believed in himself and in his ability to face a demanding and treacherous crisis. So did the citizen's of England.

We talk of confident presence in leadership. Presence does not mean a dominating, overbearing, or arrogant demeanor. It speaks to being comfortable with ourselves and true to our principles. Leaders with presence are not fearful of not having all of the answers; they have calm confidence, and don't always have to control things. They square with people on the challenges facing them and they don't duck responsibility for their decisions.

Leaders are not perfect but they all have a sense of personal efficacy that distinguishes them from those who flinch in the face of adversity. Efficacy is important to being a resilient leader. It is the ability to effectively rebound from psychological and or behavioral trouble connected to significant incidents or crises. In these situations, self-efficacy is essential—to both the leaders and the organization.

Leaders with a sense of self-efficacy believe in their ability to organize and take the action required to achieve necessary and desired goals. While it connotes confidence, it is not arrogance. Cockiness or swaggering bravado can be devoid of competence and skill, resting primarily on the emptiness of words and bluster.

Leaders believe in themselves. Beliefs influence the courses of action they pursue, the energy they put into activities, their ability to persevere in the face of obstacles and failures, and their resilience in adversity.

Churchill knew that leadership was absolutely essential in difficult times. He believed that he was placed in the Prime Minister's role at that demanding time to accomplish a particular purpose. So it is with all leaders who face crises and harsh times. Self-efficacy is not about hubris. Actually it is based in humility and holds that people, with confident optimism, can confront and prevail in turbulent times by linking people's beliefs to commitment, creativity to problems, and values to solutions.

In an interview for this book, former Senator Gary Hart was asked about what in his background gave him the confidence to believe he could be successful in government and public life. He attributed his sense of efficacy to a "strong mother," who told him as a youngster "you can do what you want to do." His parent's pride and encouragement was the source of his "early empowerment" and belief in himself. Their sacrifice and consistent support subtly helped him understand the role of determination and hard work.

As in the Senator's experience, self-efficacy is open to influence because it rests on beliefs that are and can be nurtured from childhood and from experiences confronted throughout life. "My dad always taught me to do my best," Eileen Selke, a young female superintendent said. "My father and I spent many long hours together, talking and engaged in one of his many projects such as gardening, making home-made apple cider, boiling sap from maple trees tapped out in the backyard and nearly burning down the garage—learning about what management and leadership was really about. He believed in me and I began to believe in myself."

Verbal reinforcement and encouragement—suggestions, education, and external support—affect a sense of self-efficacy. Mother's and father's bolstering words or the verbal or written expression from mentors, colleagues, or others are strong positive reinforcers. Beliefs can become strong intentions, and intentions are precursors to perseverance and courage.

Beliefs also affect a leader's thought patterns. For example, Vicktor Frankl's experience in the concentration camp accentuated the fact that "any man can come up even under such circumstances, decide what shall become of him—mentally and spiritually." Leaders do not perceive themselves as impotent victims. They have the ability to see and understand the situation, even if it's dastardly, and make a thoughtful decision on how to confront it. Even in extreme situations like Frankl's, no one can incarcerate a person's thoughts and mind.

In addition to beliefs and leaders' mental images of themselves, experience plays a big role in efficacy. Performance under pressure reinforces self-image, beliefs, and thinking. Success increases positive self-appraisal, whereas repeated failure reduces it. Failure is always disappointing, but continued and chronic failure can stymie initiative and damage self-worth. Conversely, strong and successful performance in tenuous circumstances enhances confidence to overcome hard times.

In golf, instructors advise their students to "visualize the shot." The same is true in building efficacy. Vicarious experience can help by building "future memory" that can be developed through case studies, scenario planning, or strategic thinking. Observing people performing at high levels can affect and bolster a sense of efficacy. "Seeing people like me succeed as a superintendent gave me confidence that I could do it, too," an aspiring superintendent said in a graduate seminar.

Self-efficacy builds confidence in the capability to take on tasks, work more diligently on them, and persevere in the middle of trials. In a nutshell, the greater the sense of self-efficacy leaders have, the greater their effort, persistence, and resilience.

Self-efficacy assumes, however, self-understanding and the ability to learn from personal experience and interaction with others. Good leaders are reflective and discover their personal values and act in accord with them. They also have a sense of noble goals and act in accord with the common good, not self-interest.

Efficacy translates into high goals and expectations that attract followers. High goals translate into hope and optimism. People begin to believe they can address and adapt to the difficulties they face. As we discussed in Chapter 2, optimism and hope are trademarks of resilient and confident leaders.

Leaders translate their sense of confidence to a sense of collective efficacy in the organization. A Midwestern superintendent, Gary Grant, assumed his new duties in a failing, demoralized school system of 1600 students on the periphery of a large metropolitan area. As the new superintendent, he was driving to a meeting outside the district with a veteran guidance counselor, who was also an informal leader in the district. In the course of the ride, the counselor stated, "We're glad you're here, the district isn't doing well and we need to improve. But we're a small metropolitan school district. We can only be average."

Grant listened, paused, and said, "I'm five foot seven . . . small compared to my colleagues. But I don't intend to be average. The same goes for the district. We are *not* going to be average! Our size is our largest asset." That frank optimism was the beginning of transforming that "small" district into a highly competitive one that became noted for being a personal, responsive, and creative school system.

Strong staff development, community dialogue about the schools, and the high visibility of an optimistic, energetic leader who hit the ground running with a can-do attitude became contagious. The staff worked hard and had a rebirth of the meaning in their work.

Finding fulfillment through work and helping others to do the same is motivating. Grant believed that leadership is about meaning. Applying one's skills and helping others to do the same can turn difficult situations into examples of human achievement and accomplishments. Fulfillment of noble goals gives birth to great meaning.

Personal efficacy and confidence are interwoven. Self-efficacy helps leaders persist in self-confident, energetic ways and adapt to the state of affairs to achieve goals. Resilient leaders are not beaten down by events. They have a hardiness which helps them believe that they can influence events and perceive stressful events as challenges to overcome and opportunities for growth. They act on a strong commitment to their sense of purpose and principles to help others fulfill themselves in working for the common good in tough times.

ACTION STRATEGIES TO STRENGTHEN PERSONAL EFFICACY

Action Strategy: Resilient Leaders always Try to Offset any Relative Leadership Weakness they have in an Area by Turning to others who have Strength in this Area

"Emotionally and professionally, I depended on many people that day. My colleague, Mary Pat, and I are bonded by the solder created in the tidal wave of a violent act. I leaned on her in invisible ways for support. In a quiet moment our eyes communicated what words could not clearly express. Together we faced the turmoil of that day including meeting the press," the Milwaukee area superintendent who led in heat and aftermath of a murder of a principal said. That experience exemplifies the necessity to rely on others for emotional strength as well as ideas and support.

Leadership is not about the cult of personality. It is not about charisma. It is not about the leader as savior. And, it is not about "going it alone." In difficult times, things are not always clear and leaders may not have all the skills and ability to resolve the situation by themselves.

As in the case above, successful leaders turn to others for support, to offset their weaknesses, and to prevail. Quality leaders understand that they do not have the all the answers, insight or skills; they create opportunities for collaboration and cooperation.

Building a resilient team that has a collective ability to perform under pressure is indispensable. It is a matter of respecting the talents and gifts of others and creating an environment that fosters confidence and competence. Leaders help others "fulfill themselves" in their work by encouraging them to use their skills and talent to find ways to respond to situations that seem beyond their control. They respect the capability of their team members by listening to and relying on them.

Confidence is also essential: both confidence in self and others. It takes confidence to take the advice of others and to rely on the expertise within the group, and to offset individual limitations. But leaders also build the confidence of the group to use its talent and skill. Resilient groups possess an optimistic spirit that supports them in taking initiative and persevering in difficult times. Leaders who go it alone work against the strength of the group and do not increase the capacity of the team to tackle adversity.

A symbiotic relationship exists between leaders and their colleagues. A strong team bolsters the efforts and confidence of the leader. But the leader also nurtures the confidence and capabilities of the group. Resilient leaders build confidence so individuals believe they can influence destiny even in the face of those detrimental forces and situations beyond their control.

Clint Eastwood as "Dirty Harry" said, "A man's got to know his limitations." The same is true for leaders with a sense of self-efficacy. They know their limitations and know when to seek help and rely on the abilities and perspectives of others.

Action Strategy: Resilient Leaders are always Confident that they can Learn from their Adversity to Help them be Stronger in the Future

In an idealized world, leaders never fail. One way or another, when facing adversity, the strategies and plans they implement succeed and solve the problem. Everything magically falls into place. It seems they are all-knowing and have the answers. So there is nothing they learn from the difficulties they face. They leap tall buildings in a single bound.

But life is not the movies. In science, failure is an option because most experiments do not always succeed. Through failure, information and insight are acquired, leading to potential breakthroughs. Research scientists face great adversity in trying to solve difficult and complicated issues. They are not deterred by repeated failures but use them to build the foundation for success in the future.

While it is difficult for leaders to have repeated failures and not show progress, adversity and failure happens. To say or think otherwise is not realistic. So the question to leaders is, "When you faced harsh conditions, what did you learn?"

Failure can be informative and does not have to be demoralizing. That hard nugget of failure contains information that can be used to succeed later. Resilient leaders are not married to one set of strategies or approaches; instead, they adapt to the circumstances. When they fail, they do not engage in long periods of "self-blame." Instead, they face the situation, reflect on the memories and feelings that resulted, and move ahead.

Senator Hart added a different slant on adversity. He observed that adversity is "not only a learning experience, it's also a feeling experience." The Senator asserted that by fighting the "good fight" against the odds, leaders emerged energized because they tackled something important. The rewards, Hart commented, outweigh the hazards and dangers when pursuing righteous idealism and fighting the "good fight." These efforts provide strength, energy, and confidence for leaders to persevere in the future.

Moving ahead is an important concept in building strength for the future. It means learning and growing from the past in order to pursue paths to future success. People sometimes invoke leaders facing adversity to "move on." *Moving on* implies that leaders can easily walk away from adversity, rather than face it head-on intellectually and emotionally, so they can learn and heal from it.

Therefore leaders who are shakers-turned-movers do not have to cope with their feelings in the short run. But they suppress negative memories that come back to haunt them in the long run. In a sense, leaders can "move on" and not let go of the past. They allow the stressful experience and feelings to affect their self-confidence. These feelings can be debilitating and destructive to the leadership ability to respond and make decisions, as well as cloud judgment and perspective.

As we highlighted in Chapter 1, out of disruption and adversity can emerge growth. It is more than simply "bouncing back." "Bouncing back" can mean "coming back for more" without comprehending the turmoil, adapting to what occurred, and learning new ways to approach the situation. "Getting your ears boxed off" time after time by doing the same thing in the same way in similar circumstances does not make sense. Resilience is not simply taking more unnecessary punishment. Resilient leaders are smarter than that. They learn to confront grueling conditions in a positive way.

There are many cases in history where leaders transformed tragedy and adversity into triumph and achievement. These circumstances teach us the meaning of sacrifice and determination.

Action Strategy: Resilient Leaders Maintain a Confident Presence as Leader in the Midst of Adversity

In recollecting the devastating turmoil in the aftermath of Columbine, former school superintendent Jane Hammond said that after her first press conference "someone walked up to me and said 'we need your strength.'" She embraced that challenge and stood tall as a model leader and unsung hero leading the entire community through the phases of the resilience cycle.

Demanding times frequently bring out the best in leaders. Adversity places pressure not only on leaders but also on followers. A major test of leaders is how they present themselves in the crucible of crisis when confronted with extreme difficulty. Followers want to sense a confident presence in the chaos. In these circumstances, leading is more than technical skill. It requires earning and nurturing the trust, confidence, and loyalty of the people caught in the crisis.

Studies of "leadership in extremis" undertaken by the military defined the attributes people look for in leaders during extreme circumstances. Certainly, there is no greater leadership "in extremis" than in the military where lives are at stake. But severe circumstances do not always involve life and death—they can involve intense, nonrational political or personnel situations, as well as safety and security issues.

The military studies (Kolditz, 2007) found that followers demanded leader competence, and nowhere is that more critical than in extreme contexts. No amount of legitimate or legal authority is likely to command respect or obedience in a dangerous setting. Only competence commands respect. This competence is coupled with the leader's self-confidence. Indecisiveness or a wilting presence undercuts the ability of followers to withstand and overcome the turmoil.

The military studies also concluded that leadership styles must be explicit and direct. Leaders require legitimate competence, not simply rank or organizational authority. Muddling through does not inspire confidence because followers expect demonstrated capability. This competence includes making sense of complex situations, being able to identify forces that are uncontrollable and those that can be leveraged, and strong teambuilding abilities that support their efforts.

The superintendent who led in the heat of the crisis when a principal was shot stated, "I was glazed and stunned, but paradoxically my behavior was controlled, linear, and logical. That day each decision contained a weight of incredible magnitude because of the consequences on people's lives. Time literally stood still or sped by in a vapor. It seemed surreal. For me, seconds and minutes moved in torrents and streaks, and then stagnated and the clock seemed to drag in slow motion. I don't know how I got through those first few hours. I felt removed, detached like I was having an out of body experience watching things unfold. I reacted calmly . . . I guess my experience kicked in." This story demonstrates the need for clear action grounded in a sense of presence. He knew that people would look to him for stability and strength.

Resilient leaders are not only skilled, they also are honest, have integrity, and lead by example, demonstrating confidence and self-control. In crises they do not see themselves as victims, but demonstrate the character to believe they are "response-able" and able to respond in a competent and trust-worthy manner because others depend on it. They don't stand by, wringing their hands, and blaming others for their misfortune. They find ways to respond to challenges and persevere, prevail, and grow.

Resilient leaders reduce panic and increase the confidence of the people with whom they work. Confident leaders develop the pride and build organizational efficacy, inspiring others to believe they can respond and succeed in unfortunate situations.

Action Strategy: Resilient Leaders always take a Deliberate, Step-by-Step Approach to Overcome Adversity

Most definitions of leadership contain the idea of social influence, more aptly defined as the ability to inspire individuals to do things they otherwise might not be inclined to do. Leaders communicate a sense of hope and optimism and define what can be done in tough situations to achieve results.

Credibility is reinforced and strengthened by actions and the decisions made in a variety of circumstances. Certainly, this has to do with self-confidence but it also speaks to how leaders respond and behave in overcoming turbulent events. In stressful situations, resilient leaders take a considered approach to deal with issues. They:

- Do not wait to respond. They attend to the situation and approach leadership as an active, not passive, role.
- Do not focus on mistakes, failures, or complaints. They work to devise solutions.
- Do not avoid decisions. Decisions can invoke action or can deter actions. Either can be detrimental to the organization or individuals. Knowing when and how to act, and knowing when and how not to respond, requires intelligence and wisdom.

Serious and ambiguous situations require conscious, clear, and deliberate decision-making. Knee-jerk responses can explode and make situations worse. Crisis requires a calm, problem-centered approach that considers diverse strategies.

Sometimes, linear, rational problem-solving approaches are required, and at other times more intuitive approaches are called for because logic may not rule and information is not available. Intuitive decisions are not guesswork. Leaders with intuition have a deep understanding of their job through experience, content, and conceptual knowledge. They can see how the "pieces" fit together and the effect of the intangible dynamics.

The world is not always a rational place that succumbs to cause-and-effect logic. Leaders know how to create and follow a coherent strategy, but they also know how and when to improvise. Improvisation is not just "winging it," guesswork or panic reactions. Seasoned leaders know when to deviate from plans and established processes. Data do not always tell the whole story or may be unavailable. When time is of the essence, intuitive improvisation implemented clearly may be the most deliberate course of action. Leaders make the most of whatever resources are available to get the job done. But there is an order to improvising solutions.

School administrators, like other leaders, are disciplined. They are tight around values and ethics but flexible around procedures. Values and principles set the limits for improvisation or for any action for that matter. Improvisational strategies must fit the organization's culture and values.

After tough decisions are made under tough circumstances, resilient leaders take a deliberate, step-by-step approach to reflect on the impact of the decisions. They ask questions such as:

- Was the problem solved?
- Did the decision create unexpected consequences that could lead to great advantages?
- Did the strategy destroy the integrity of the organization [did the means justify the ends]?
- What new learning or unique slant on the issue caused us to think differently?
- Did we increase the efficiency of the organization by getting things done quicker?

Focusing on effective problem solving, and not getting mired in defensive or hasty decisions, requires a leader with confidence and courage. They examine the bigger picture, determine the stakes at hand and the meaning of the situation, and then proceed in a step-by-step manner to implement their decision.

Action Strategy: Resilient Leaders Demonstrate the Essential Knowledge and Skills to Lead in Tough Times

Adversity brings out the best in leaders. It requires skill, depth of knowledge, and a conceptual understanding of the bigger picture in order to make sense of the situation. Confident leaders believe they have the personal strength and resources to meet adversity and chaos. They also have the ability to work with others effectively.

As a result, these leaders set challenging goals, calmly face the difficulty, work harder, and actively search for effective strategies and solutions. As we said earlier, they solicit and find information, and share viewpoints and perceptions with others so that they can help others and respond to what is happening. Building strong informal leadership is very important in overcoming adversity. People see and need leaders as a source of information and ideas for addressing the turmoil.

A school administrator from Massachusetts, David Kleinhorst, confronted a disastrous fire that totally destroyed a school. He had to follow most of the steps just mentioned in not only managing the immediacy of the crisis but also planning for the longer term. "I had to convey a sense of confidence and optimism." Kleinhorst said, "The people looked to me for direction." His team and members of the community had confidence in his ability because of his past track record. He always addressed tough issues, not ignored them. Using his management and interpersonal skills, he worked with the community through the first weeks of the crisis, found a solution for the immediate future, and then worked on a new facility.

Kleinhorst modeled the action strategy of demonstrating confidence and competence. He:

- Made decisions and recommendations despite not having as much information as desired.
- Summarized their perspective on the situation at a moment's notice.
- Navigated a fine line between over-informing and under-informing others about the situation and the nature of the work.
- Relayed critical information to others, even if they did not request it.
- Assessed the likely political ramifications of actions.
- Estimated the damage that may incur as a result of decisions to act or not to act.

When times are routine, leadership is not vital. Confident leadership in difficult times absolutely *is* vital. Senator Hart indicated that leaders with the knowledge and skill can "get out in front" of situations and use their creative ability, skill, and knowledge to take advantage of difficult situations to find new ways and make productive changes.

Finally, in overcoming adversity, resilient leadership serves as a beacon. Cursing the darkness of adversity is futile, but in hard times, light, in the form of new opportunities and learning, may help imaginative solutions blossom. Adversity can uncover subtle nuances that provide new perspectives for positive advances. Growth is seldom a painless and risk-free process, because it is difficult to give up old thinking patterns and mindsets.

SUMMARY

Pressure and turmoil are a part of leadership. The true challenge, however, is developing a sense of efficacy in the ability to contribute and meet the challenge. That is when leadership assumes its deepest meaning.

The educational leader at Columbine discovered that the tragedy "built on my skills that I was developing as an administrator. I learned that I had the ability to deal with the issues and be steady and not panic and move through the situation. I depended on an inner circle of colleagues because I know I couldn't do it on my own."

Crisis and adversity compel the need for strong and decisive leaders—those who demonstrate the competence and confidence to define the issues, stand tall with resolve, mobilize people, and visualize a better tomorrow. In this chapter we outlined specific strategies that leaders can implement so they can strengthen their confidence and competence in tough times.

CHARTING YOUR RESILIENCE PROFILE FOR PERSONAL EFFICACY

To chart your Leader Resilience Profile for *Personal Efficacy,* return to your completed LRP Survey in Chapter 1, then follow these steps:

- For each item number listed, circle your *actual* item response on the chart.
- Determine the *conversion* score for the item, located directly beneath the *actual* number you circled.
- Enter your conversion score in the box on the extreme right column of the chart.
- Sum the scores in the right column to determine your Resilience Strength Score for *Personal Efficacy.*
- Observe your individualized score on the continuum from Moderately Low to Very High.

Table 4.1. Personal Efficacy Subscale

Strength: Personal Efficacy

Item #	Item Response							Enter your Conversion Score for the Item
2	If your *actual* item response is: Then your *conversion* score is: **enter your conversion score in the box →**	1 1	2 2	3 3	4 4	5 5	6 6	
20	If your *actual* item response is: Then your *conversion* score is: **enter your conversion score in the box →**	1 6	2 5	3 4	4 3	5 2	6 1	
48	If your *actual* item response is: Then your *conversion* score is: **enter your conversion score in the box →**	1 6	2 5	3 4	4 3	5 2	6 1	
53	If your *actual* item response is: Then your *conversion* score is: **enter your conversion score in the box →**	1 1	2 2	3 3	4 4	5 5	6 6	
58	If your *actual* item response is: Then your *conversion* score is: **enter your conversion score in the box →**	1 6	2 5	3 4	4 3	5 2	6 1	
63	If your *actual* item response is: Then your *conversion* score is: **enter your conversion score in the box →**	1 1	2 2	3 3	4 4	5 5	6 6	
						Strength Score: Efficacy →		

Strength Score Continuum for Personal Efficacy

Resilience Level →	Moderately Low	Moderate	Moderately High	Very High
Score Range →	13–18	19–24	25–30	31–36

Chapter 5

Support for Leaders in Turbulent Times

When crisis conditions erupt, it can bring leaders to their emotional knees unless they have a strong and viable support base. Ironically, though, support is not always sought or offered. In their book, *Lonely at the Top,* Jazzar and Kimball (2004) reported that today's tumultuous times leave leaders feeling more isolated and vulnerable than ever, without a support base to rely on. And leaders who try to create a support base after crisis strikes have waited too late. Preparation for anticipated but unseen adversity is therefore critical. Establishing a support base network during relatively normal times can provide the foundation necessary to survive and even grow stronger from adversity.

Our intent in this chapter is to provide guidance for leaders who want to strengthen their resilience in this area. We begin by examining why leaders feel so lonely at the top. We then turn to action strategies leaders can implement to meet their needs for direction, emotional comfort, and a safe haven in tough times.

LONELY LEADERS

The organizational structure of schools and school districts isolates leaders. Faculty, staff, students, and parents regard the school leader as someone rather removed from their own day-to-day existence. School leaders, whether feared or revered, organizationally are set apart from the rest. Wheatley (2007) observed, "Pioneering leaders face very challenging conditions. They act in isolation, are often criticized, mocked, or ignored by the prevailing culture "(p.167). One of the reasons for this predicament is the curse of the job. The leader's perceived power and influence, real or imagined, puts the leader on a different plane in the organizational pecking order. Even the community puts them there. Wheatley (2007) weighed in with this rather harsh conclusion, "Society does not want them to succeed. If we acknowledge their success, it means we will have to change. We will have to abandon the comfort of our familiar beliefs and practices. Even as the old ways fail, we hold onto them more fiercely and apply them more zealously" (p. 169).

Another contributing factor to the loneliness is an aura of mystique that surrounds many leaders. According to Jazzar and Kimball (2004), many people are either frightened or intimidated by someone in authority or are unwilling to try to get to know the leader as a human being. Think of times in your own leadership role where people you serve seemed surprised, even shocked, to catch you in dirty clothes on a weekend doing yard chores. Elementary principals have to answer their young students' queries like this one during a Saturday trip to the supermarket, "What are you doing here? Why aren't you back at my school?" Examples such as these reflect how others tend to perceive leaders as not "real" people.

A third reason for loneliness at the top can be attributed to leaders themselves. Some leaders have been taught by example that true leaders "go it alone." The Lone Ranger Complex develops when leaders believe that they show weakness, not strength, if they need to lean on a support base. So they tell themselves, "I can handle it. I don't need any help." Then they act accordingly, reinforcing the feeling among the followers that leaders seem aloof, not relating to the followers. In addition, our individualistic culture in the United States reinforces the stereotype of the independent leader who exhibits self-reliant strength and resolve.

Because of these factors, leaders may be prone to set aside the experience others have to offer. Don Moyer (2009), writing in the Harvard Business Review, noted that English author and humorist Douglas Adams said, "Human beings, who are almost unique in having the ability to learn from the experience of others, are also remarkable for their apparent disinclination to do so" (p. 120). Moyer commented, "Despite the power of learning first-hand, the lessons experience offers can sometimes be misleading." He also on cautioned that, "Leaders should be aware of this as they move up through an organization and into increasingly demanding roles. Wisdom may come from experience, but mere wisdom isn't always enough to tackle the complicated challenges facing today's senior managers" (p. 120).

Leaders must recognize that seeking the advice of others does not signal weakness. On the contrary, it demonstrates a leader's reasoned understanding of how important it is to draw upon valuable resources as they are needed.

Leaders have to ask themselves why they would go it alone when there are many resources readily available to deal with adversity.

It gets even lonelier over time as leaders cumulatively make tough decisions that run counter to the interests, preferences, and wishes of the followers. Former superintendent Dave Watson had a formula for this phenomenon. He called it the 10% rule. Each year a leader may lose up to 10% of his or her support because of difficult leadership decisions that are made. At the end of five years, Watson calculated, 50% are for the leader and 50% percent are against, it may be high time to get back on the horse and ride out of town (Jazzar and Kimbal, 2004, p.12).

Most certainly, there will be periods of adversity for all leaders, periods when they cannot rely on the organization as a system for support. It is during these times leaders must call upon their support base to help replenish the emotional losses adversity can extract. We choose the term *must* deliberately. Recall from our discussion in Chapter 1 that the skill set of capacity building is the fuel tank for becoming more resilient in the face of the storm. This energy, however, is only dormant potential. The skill set becomes useless, in a practical sense, if leaders do not actively take the steps necessary to strengthen their support base *before* adversity strikes. In the balance of this chapter we discuss specific strategies to replenish and refuel the resilience capacity of leaders.

ACTION STRATEGIES TO STRENGTHEN LEADER SUPPORT BASE

Action Strategy: Resilient Leaders Learn from the Professional Experiences of others who Faced Similar Circumstances

Leaders can tap a wealth of experience in their field if they make the effort to seek out other, more senior leaders. There are few types of circumstances a leader can encounter that other leaders have not already faced. Of course, careful consideration should be given to who is sought for advice. Who does the leader know who has led similar organizations and has faced similar adversity? With whom can the leader have a trusting relationship to the extent that she or he feels comfortable sharing doubts and fears? Who among the leader's acquaintances can serve as a good role model? And, with whom can the leader feel comfortable sharing small successes achieved during adversity? These are critical considerations that, if addressed now, over time can result in the establishment of a strong base for support and an added measure of resilience when adversity strikes.

New leaders should make every effort to cultivate relationships with experienced leaders within the region. A school administrator in New England supported this view. When asked where his professional support base came from, he responded, "My colleague administrators. I have always found it rewarding to be a part of this group at the local, state and national level. I would tell anyone who finds themselves in a leadership position that we all have a lot to benefit from talking to one another." Developing a cadre of "go to" leaders and knowing who can be most helpful under given circumstances can provide leaders with an advantage when adversity looms. Regular and frequent conversation with experienced leaders can help the new leader see the elements of adversity as they are forming, making it possible to move more swiftly through the low points in the resilience cycle described in Chapter 1.

It is often said that experience is the best teacher. Certainly the second best teacher is watching the best. There is so much to learn from leaders who have successfully dealt with adversity in the past. As Stone emphasized (2007), "Any discussion of how to boost performance of staff must include mentoring." In our own interviews with leaders, most pointed to one or more individuals who had a major influence in their professional lives. Mary Anne Prince, Superintendent in a Northeast suburban district, gave a lot of credit to others for her success in tough times, "Most of it comes from having strong role models both professionally and personally; personally with the message you can do it, there are no limits; professionally from watching other superintendents, other close friends, colleagues. Joe taught me more of what I could do and not do than anybody else. You could stand back and say I can see where he is going, see why he is doing it."

David Domm, a very successful leader nationally, reinforced this point, "I was a superintendent at 33 and I knew there was a lot I did not know and I took it upon myself to go to senior superintendents for advice, to go to business partners and ask to participate in their training." During these sessions there is often the opportunity to engage directly and personally with role models. The nature of the educational leadership culture makes it comfortable for open exchange of issues and ideas among and between beginner and experienced experts.

Another professional support base is cultivated through networking. Every opportunity should be taken to be in close proximity with other leaders, such as at conferences, regional and local administrator meetings, staff development activities, and when possible direct personal contact. Megan Frey, a superintendent in upstate New York advised, "I think that one of the most valuable pieces is to be able to network. Pick up the phone and call a seasoned veteran. There is no one else that understands better than fellow administrators." Some leaders new to leadership react negatively to this suggestion because they view networking as synonymous with politicking. Understandably, there are times when the politics of self-interest are work in the motivation to network. We argue that self-interest is o.k. as long as it is not the driving motive for building bridges. We view networking as reaching out across the boundaries of the district and community to a broader basis of possible support.

Action Strategy: Resilient Leaders have the Resources of a Strong Personal Support Base to Help them through Tough Times in their Leadership Role

A personal support base can be erected on a number of support pillars, including friends, family, clergy, and specific support groups. Friends may not have an understanding about the pressure the leader faces and the tough decisions the leader is compelled to make on a regular basis, but friends can provide a very important diversion from the pressure cooker environment of the job. They can provide a safe, nonjudgmental haven of support. The haven can be as varied as the golf course, the bowling lanes, or the bridge group. One veteran leader summarized the sentiments of colleagues leaders when he pointed to the fact that socializing with friends let him be who he is without title, power, and the baggage that accompanies a leadership role.

Family can serve in much the same role but with the added, important component of love. Jay Dunbar, a Florida superintendent, talked about the stress he encountered from divided school board factions in his pursuit of a superintendent's position in their district. Dunbar's support came from his family, "My family will stand behind me no matter what. When I went through this search it was a pretty out of control search. They would call me every day to see what was going on." They do not care about your work decisions. They care about you. Anna Beam, Assistant Superintendent in the Northeast, said, "My husband is my best friend and that has been my source of strength. I am not a person to turn to others. I take care of my personal issues, with help from my husband along the way."

Jane Morehouse turned to her parents for inspirational support, "My mom and dad were not college educated. So I knew that hard work was what they did and got them through. That value of hard work is part of who I am." Another school leader said he drew strength from parents in a different way, "I had exceptionally good role models in them and I remember their lessons so vividly. They're both gone now but there really isn't a day that goes by that I don't remember something they did and the way they did it."

Renita Vega, the owner of a school in Mexico just south of San Diego, faced an unexpected crisis in the form of a previous owner attempting to seize the school property because it was demonstrating such success, academically and financially. He exerted his political muscle through intimidation, bribes, and other illegal measures to gain control of Vega's school. The previous owner's relentless attacks lasted for eight years. Vega recounted to us that her support base of family and religious faith were indispensible in her eventual success after years of pain.

Vegas expanded the typical definition of family to include the family within the school, "Our close employees, the principal, dean of students, and the teachers who have been with us for at least five or six years and have lived with me through this ordeal were an incredible base of support." Vega continued, "I told my husband while crying that maybe we needed to go through this so that we could really understand how much these individuals love the school, love us, and love what we are doing." She concluded by saying that she was so blessed by this support that she forgot about the horror of what she was experiencing.

We should note that not all leaders agree that family is a primary source to rely on in times of adversity, particularly the daily grind and stresses of the job. As one leader summarized this perspective, "I get paid the big bucks to take the abuses of this job. My family doesn't get paid a penny. I am not going to burden them with my work crises." Other leaders described in emotional detail the pain to the family. For example, a high school principal talked about the mistreatment of his son who was a student at the high school. "One teacher told David she was not going to let him participate at the upcoming National Debate Tournament because other teachers would accuse her of playing favorites. I might add that David was the top debater at school. Another time, students who were not selected for Advanced Placement programs blamed David for taking their spots. They said in no uncertain terms the only reason he was in AP courses was because of his father. I didn't know about these instances until after David graduated. He said he didn't want me to be upset, even though I am sure the episodes upset him tremendously." Regardless of the extent that leaders choose to bring home the crises at work, family almost always offers a safe haven, providing respite from the anguish of leadership.

Clergy and the church also serve an important role for the leaders we interviewed. In the next chapter we expand on the broader context of spirituality as a support base. For now we want to highlight the importance of people connected by their faith. Lou Anne Ray told us that all of her life she has been influenced by wisdom offered by her pastor. "He said that life was like a long hall full of doors on each side. As you go down the hall, you will try to go through some doors and they will remain closed. Other doors will open more easily and that is God's way of guiding you. You need to follow the opening of opportunities presented." Ray applied this message when she was being politically forced from an administrative position. "This door had just slammed shut in my face and there was no sense trying to go through it. There was nothing more I could do." So Ray, heeding the advice from her pastor, turned to her support base of networks and that led her to a new position full of challenges.

Another support base can be found in formal or informal support groups formed for a specific purpose. A former suburban superintendent outside of Boston offered this example of a professional support group, "A group of about ten superintendents in the surrounding area realized that we needed a safe place to go to help us with the adversity all of us were experiencing. So we agreed to share the costs of having a trained psychologist facilitate discussions on a monthly basis. This lasted for several years and was a tremendous support to all of us." This is a clear example of leaders collectively assuming personal responsibility for finding ways to help them strengthen their resilience capacity of support base.

Adversity in a leader's personal life can siphon resilience energy in the professional role as well. Two women school administrators we talked with provided concrete examples of how they drew on support to help them through personal tragedy. As an assistant superintendent in the Southeast, Jane Morehouse described the source of her strength as she dealt with breast cancer, "It was the most heart-warming experience to walk back into that school and see the kind of support I had." Retired New York Board of Cooperative Education Services District Superintendent, Bea Outland, another cancer survivor, revealed the importance of seeking support from those who have walked a similar path before,

> The term "survival" took on new meaning. I knew that death could be in my future, but then death is part of all our futures, so no sense wasting time and energy there. Recovery and restoring wellness became my focus. I read and read. I talked with many people about their experience with cancer and I suddenly realized that I was talking with them because they were all survivors!

Her revelation captures advice every leader should heed: Seek out those who have been there before you. Find and relate to those who have survived adversity you face. It may help to put what you face in the proper perspective relative to what others have faced and survived. Most leaders are not born resilient; they must learn to bring together those people upon whom they can rely to provide an emotional base of support. As one school leader reflected on his support base, "If they are there for you, it makes far less difference if others are against you."

Action Strategy: Resilient Leaders never Hesitate to Tell those they Trust about their Doubts or Fears Related to Adversity

Keeping it all inside can only serve to further deepen the leader's feelings of isolation during times of adversity. It can harden the leader's perspective, narrowing her or his sense of the options available to deal with the issues. Sharing those doubts and fears with others signals a willingness to receive constructive feedback. The feedback can broaden the base of applicable ideas and viewpoints that can both ease the burden and provide new approaches and solutions that may not have been considered. What appeared particularly troublesome now became manageable. Armed with the support and some fresh ideas from others, things may seem far less daunting than before.

Lou Anne Ray faced double jeopardy when both a personal and professional crisis struck at the same time. On the professional front, she was informed that, due to a change in governors, her senior administrative position was being eliminated, just one year after she moved across the nation to accept the position. At the same time she faced, in her words, "the largest personal crisis I had ever confronted in my life that had serious family repercussions. All of this happened at once. I really thought I was going crazy. I didn't know if I was going to survive this." And Ray was emotionally and physically alone in an unfamiliar state.

But she didn't allow herself to wallow in the victim status very long. "I picked up the phone and called my friend Renita in California. She dropped everything she was doing and rushed to be with me." Upon Renita's arrival, Ray bombarded her with doubts and fears, "How could I not have seen this coming? Am I that naïve as a person?" Together they spent the week working through Ray's emotions. "She made sure that I didn't hit the bottom to the point that I couldn't get back up and put myself together again."Ray summarized her thoughts about the support base of friends, "It's about having a person in your personal life who is not a family member and who is a resilient person herself. When she told me 'you're going to be able to get through this and be successful,' I believed she knew what she was talking about because she has successfully moved through tremendous difficulties."

Leaders may feel that sharing doubts and fears is a sign of weakness. Realistically, leaders simply cannot have all of the answers nor can they expect to always be fully confident in the face of a new, never seen before crisis. Reaching out to others in times of adversity can reinforce the leader's resolve. Words of encouragement from trusted colleagues and advice from mentors can do much to overcome the anxiety that can accompany adversity. Opening up to another person, sharing one's deepest doubts and fears, should only be done with someone who can be trusted to honor confidentiality and truly understands the vulnerability the leader feels.

Action Strategy: Resilient Leaders are always Comfortable Sharing with their Support Base any Small Wins they Achieve along the Road to Recovering from Adversity

Success should be shared for at least two important reasons. First, sharing reinforces the experience. However small a success might seem during a time of adversity, it represents a very significant emotional victory. It should be celebrated accordingly. Sometimes it may seem petty, through the lens of the school leader, to tell others about small steps forward in moving through the resilience cycle. Researchers have shown, however, the mere act of voicing a success makes it seem more real to the person talking about it. And it feels good to acknowledge successes, however small they may seem.

An elementary principal in the deep South, Dante Miche, commented that he felt comfortable talking to his partner at home about, in his words, "the little bitty steps I have taken to win over the trust of the staff." The principal was new to the school, arriving in the wake of a departing, dearly beloved principal of twenty-eight years. The staff did not want the principal for reasons that weren't professionally based. But the small steps, such as the staff agreeing to meet at Miche's home for dinner to celebrate the school's performance on state performance exams, was a large breakthrough in principal-staff relationships. And it was helpful for Miche to be able to share with his partner the pride he felt in this accomplishment.

Second, supporters can use their awareness of the small victories to remind and reinforce the leader's efforts to deal with adversity in the future. It is easy for the leader to fail to recall past success when there are still obstacles in the way. For example, two years into the job, Principal Miche was still not trusted by a handful of teachers. When Miche lapsed into self-pity over this, his partner say factually, "But, Dante, look how far you have come in two years with the rest of the staff. Don't be so hard on yourself. Even though you aren't home free yet, you have plenty of reasons be proud of all you have accomplished in a short time."

Most leaders would agree that today's tumultuous times bring greater stress to leadership roles than any other times in recent memory. Looking to the future, support becomes even more crucial. And one of the leaders we interviewed expressed concern about the sources of this support, "A concern that I have is that people are substituting cyberspace for face to face human connections in relationships. I happen to believe that these relationships are critical to face the challenges that we are confronted with over our long careers. I worry that many of our newer administrators don't see the value of those professional relationships." Kelso summarized how this challenge affects all administrators, "The challenge we face as a profession is how to nurture the relationships so that our upcoming leaders have supportive people in and around their lives to help them become more resilient and weather the storms." Our intent in this chapter was to provide concrete action strategies to help address the challenge that Kelso issued.

SUMMARY

This chapter began with the recognition that leaders claim and research documents that leaders serve in roles that can be very lonely at times, a condition that worsens when heavy-duty adversity hits. We strongly urged leaders to let go of the temptation to go it alone. This approach only exacerbates the isolation and loneliness leaders reported. We described with real-life examples how leaders have developed and sustained a strong support base to call upon in times of trouble. Friends, colleagues, mentors, family, clergy, and professional networks all stand ready to assist. In the final section, we examined specific strategies that leaders have used to build their valuable support system to help them survive, and even thrive, on the other end of adversity.

CHARTING YOUR RESILIENCE PROFILE FOR LEADER SUPPORT BASE

To chart your Leader Resilience Profile for *Leader Support Base,* return to your completed LRP Survey in Chapter 1, then follow these steps:

- For each item number listed, circle your *actual* item response on the chart.
- Determine the *conversion* score for the item, located directly beneath the *actual* number you circled.
- Enter your conversion score in the box on the extreme left of the chart.
- Sum the scores in the left column to determine your Resilience Strength Score for *Leader Support Base.*
- Observe your individualized score on the continuum from Moderately Low to Very High.

Table 5.1. Support Base Subscale

Strength: Support Base

Item #	Item Response							Enter your Conversion Score for the Item
8	If your *actual* item response is:	1	2	3	4	5	6	
	Then your *conversion* score is:	1	2	3	4	5	6	
	enter your conversion score in the box →							
14	If your *actual* item response is:	1	2	3	4	5	6	
	Then your *conversion* score is:	1	2	3	4	5	6	
	enter your conversion score in the box →							
27	If your *actual* item response is:	1	2	3	4	5	6	
	Then your *conversion* score is:	1	2	3	4	5	6	
	enter your conversion score in the box →							
68	If your *actual* item response is:	1	2	3	4	5	6	
	Then your *conversion* score is:	6	5	4	3	2	1	
	enter your conversion score in the box →							
70	If your *actual* item response is:	1	2	3	4	5	6	
	Then your *conversion* score is:	1	2	3	4	5	6	
	enter your conversion score in the box →							
73	If your *actual* item response is:	1	2	3	4	5	6	
	Then your *conversion* score is:	6	5	4	3	2	1	
	enter your conversion score in the box →							
	Strength Score: Support Base →							

Strength Score for Support Base

Resilience Level →	Moderately Low	Moderate	Moderately High	Very High
Score Range →	13–18	19–24	25–30	31–36

Chapter 6

The Personal Well-Being
of Leaders

Aspiring leaders learn rather early in their leadership preparation programs that effective leadership is organic, not mechanical. The *wholeness* of leading is greater than the sum of its discrete, mechanical parts. What prospective leaders don't always learn in their training is that ESP is part of the organic whole. In this chapter we refer to a different kind of ESP, the Emotional, Spiritual, and Physical well-being of leaders. These elements interact to shape the overall health and resilience of leaders.

Even though we consider ESP well-being to be organic, for discussion purposes in this chapter we also spend time on each element separately. First we begin with a discussion of emotional well-being as a construct, and then we provide concrete action strategies to help leaders become stronger in this area. We apply this pattern in subsequent discussion about spiritual and physical well-being. We conclude the chapter with an action strategy to address time, a universal problem that directly affects leaders' overall sense of personal well-being as well as their resilience capacity.

EMOTIONAL WELL-BEING

Daniel Goleman (1995) popularized and extended earlier seminal research on the emotional well-being of people, or what he referred to as emotional intelligence. Researchers have examined the significance of emotional intelligence by looking at four components of the construct (Mayer, Salovey, & Caruso, 2000):

Perceiving emotions: the ability to perceive emotions in oneself and others accurately; *using emotions to facilitate thought:* the capacity to integrate emotions in thought and to use emotions in a way that facilitates cognitive processes; *understanding emotions:* the capacity to understand emotional concept and meanings, the links between emotions and the relationships they signal; and *managing emotions:* the capacity to monitor and regulate emotions for personal and social growth and well-being. (pp. 396–420)

Substantial research in support of these components makes it possible to examine how they influence resilience strategies and overall well-being of leaders (Mayer, Salovey, & Caruso, 2000).

The first component is *accurately perceiving emotions in oneself and others.* Goleman (1995) noted that Socrates' injunction "know thyself" speaks to this keystone of emotional intelligence: awareness of one's own feelings as they occur. It is the ability to accurately identify personal emotions such as, "I'm very angry right now," or "I'm very disappointed right now." Additionally, it is the ability to accurately identify the emotional state of others, using facial and nonverbal cues as well as verbal cues during an interaction. If emotions are not read correctly either in self or others, then managing the emotions becomes a moot issue

The second component is *using emotion to facilitate thought.* Our emotional interpretation of events can be dramatically changed by changing the emotional color of the glasses through which we see the events transpire. Emotion can rise and fall within us in a fast and imprecise fashion. Different parts of our brain with different functions influence our emotional and rational thought (Goleman, 1995). In fact, Goleman talked about "neural hijacking" where negative and positive emotions can change our rational problem solving processes, sometimes for the better and sometimes for the worse (p. 14). In Chapter 2 we outlined two dimensions of resilience thinking skills: understanding reality and envisioning a positive future. Along with their thinking skills, resilient leaders call upon their resilience emotional skills to help them reframe a difficult situation in a more positive light. An example that exemplifies this process is to always expect that good things can come out of an adverse situation. Leaders must be mindful to acknowledge the difficult aspects and emotions associated with an adverse situation. However, leaders who approach a negative situation with a positive attitude for problem solving demonstrate resilience in leadership.

Consider the following observation by a school leader we interviewed, "It all starts with attitude. If you translate setbacks into losses and defeats, it's very difficult to come back quickly. For example, we just had a large bond vote fail and my message was 'Yes, it was disappointing, but we weren't discouraged.' Did we want it to go forward? Yes we did! We did understand also that people had a lot of different perspectives on it. We weren't discouraged because we had new information that would help us go back and retool it, so that when we brought it out again it would be something the whole community could support." Emotional resilience is part of the filter that sees possibilities rather than discouragements during difficult situations.

The third component is *understanding the meaning of emotions*. To maintain stability and consistency of progress during the challenges of change, leaders must be able to sense and gauge emotional climate and reactions of themselves, their staff, and their community. One resilience strategy that supports this effort is for leaders to demonstrate an understanding of their own emotions during adversity and how these emotions affect their leadership performance. Schilling (2008) commented that, "People in the workplace have feelings and emotions—and we should deal with them by first dealing with our own" (p. 19). Especially during adversity, leaders need to be able to identify what they are feeling as well as how those feelings may interfere with their ability to be objective and move ahead.

The fourth component is *managing emotions in self and others*. The skills to identify and understand the meaning of emotions are building blocks to the skill of managing one's own emotions as well as those of others. According to Goleman (1995), this is the crux of emotional intelligence. He referred to this as the "meta-ability" that determines how well leaders perform. Truly resilient leaders demonstrate the ability to assess and react to feelings attached to situations and problems while they cooperatively build strategies to move forward in positive directions.

An educational leader we interviewed reflected on how he came to understand his emotions stimulated by adversity and how he changed from naive to knowledgeable in this regard, especially his reactions over time to negative things that have happened to good people. "When I was younger, surprises came in bunches. And you learn that although you try and always do the right thing that bad things will still happen to good people. This is one of the liabilities of having been raised a little too much Catholic. You have a consequence driven life. And, basically, you are taught early on that if you do the right thing, right things happen. But that's absolutely not the case, and I was completely unprepared emotionally for this experience." The understanding of the meanings of his emotions during these unexpected adverse situations allowed him to become emotionally prepared for similar experiences he has dealt with throughout his educational leadership career.

ACTION STRATEGIES TO STRENGTHEN
PERSONAL WELL-BEING

Using the four functions as a base we now turn our attention to leadership strategies that strengthen the emotional well-being of leaders.

Action Strategy: Resilient Leaders Emotionally Accept those Things they Cannot Influence in a Positive Way

This strategy underscores an important element of the Serenity Prayer, "Grant me the serenity to accept things that I cannot change, courage to change the things I can, and wisdom to know the difference." The wisdom to know the difference is tied directly to resilience capacity. Leaders who don't discern the difference when they are mired in a particular set of adverse circumstances end up draining their resilience capacity trying to fix things beyond their control. This strategy is not the same as giving up, nor is it an indicator of impotence to act in a negative situation. Rather, this skill allows resilient leaders to get beyond the negative aspects of a situation to identify those aspects that can be worked with. As one educational leader explained it, it's coming to terms with the reality that you are not likely going to change the skeptics and cynics who reject your leadership direction.

Another educational leader summarized this strategy more succinctly, "Develop a thick skin." Mary Schmidt, former superintendent from Ohio, described her reaction to attacks directed at her, "It took me a long time to develop the thick skin and not go home and cry about them." A colleague administrator expressed similar sentiments, "Do I get stressed? Of course, but . . . emotionally it does not take a toll on me when I am doing the right thing and can clarify my actions." Events that educational leaders deal with can get very emotionally tense and nasty, requiring them to monitor themselves so that other staff in the situation learn by example to manage their own emotions. A leader described it this way, "They would watch me, in a room where people were screaming and yelling sometimes very hurtful things, just accept it. I try to not emotionalize and personalize. I try very hard to intellectualize when I'm in moments that are extremely hurtful, but that's really hard to do."

Followers hang onto every word and gesture by leaders, looking for cues about how to spend their emotional intelligence. David Cottrell (2007) reinforced this point to leaders, "Everything you do matters because your team is watching . . . and depending on you to do the right thing" (p. 49). Leadership teams observe how leaders cope with adversity emotionally and intellectually, and they generally will respond accordingly if
leaders exhibit a calm focus during tough times.

Action Strategy: Resilient Leaders Emotionally Let Go of any Goal they are Pursuing if it's Causing them to Sacrifice more Important Long-term Goals and Values

This strategy is not the same as acting like a quitter, taking one's toys away and going somewhere else to play. This strategy is in some ways a strategy of last resort. It is applicable when leaders realize, after concerted efforts and lots of anguish, that continued pursuit of a goal is not worth the cost paid to higher order values, exacting too much of a cost personally and to family.

Lou Anne Ray rose through the ranks in her large, urban school district to an assignment as Assistant Superintendent. When the superintendent retired and a new leader was hired from out of district, he brought his deputy superintendent with him and promptly relegated Ray to his assistant for all things boring. In her words, "I was his maid in waiting. I had to be at the office until late at night playing secretary for him and making name tags for meetings." Ray said her self esteem suffered until a culminating blow forced her to make a tough decision. "One evening I was sitting by his side, taking notes during a meeting with his leadership group and he lost the button on his coat. He picks up the button, places it on my computer and directs me to sew the button on this coat before the next meeting. He did that publicly in front of my colleagues who comprise the leadership team I served on until his regime." Ray said that incident was the pivotal point for her to conclude she could not stay in that position.

In this example, Ray gave up on the hope she would ever find importance and self esteem in her job as unilaterally redefined. In order to preserve her own integrity, a higher order value to her than loyalty to the superintendent, she left the district for an assignment where she regained her sense of self efficacy.

Another school leader described crisis adversity that demonstrated the fragility of emotional resilience in the organization. Sam Greene, a Virginia school administrator, shared the following: "The bomb threats were difficult to take because they got at our core value of a safe environment for kids to learn. And that was probably emotionally the most difficult, because we can't make people feel safe when we can't catch the people who are doing it. The impact on the high school administrative staff was devastating. We reached a point after so many threats when I'd never seen such despair in our administrative team. I had a couple of the administrators who were crying, because they felt so helpless. Then you know that the goals that you have to achieve that year are never going to happen if the emotional state of the people who have to implement them with you is so precarious. So you put those goals on hold and say, alright, I've got to deal with rebuilding the resilience of my administrative staff before we're going to get to anything else accomplished." Sometimes when crisis happens, leaders have to regroup and refocus for a while before moving forward. Not only does this maintain their own capacity for resilience, but it replenishes the capacity of their leadership teams as well.

Action Strategy: Resilient Leaders Stay in Touch with their Emotions During Adversity and Realize how their Emotions Affect their Leadership Performance

Leaders are always under close scrutiny said Mary Kay Collan, a school leader in California. But in times of extreme turmoil the way leaders perform has heightened and long lasting impact. At any given moment the situation may seem hopeless, but it is also probable that there will be an eventual resolution of the issue. In the aftermath of crisis, if the leader's performance was measured, emotionally managed and constructive, the future positive impact of that conduct will pay dividends. One leader called upon a mantra from his family to emotionally guide him through challenging events in his school: "My mother always used to say while we were growing up, 'Be the person you'd be proud to be' . . . that thought went through my head dozens of times every day. Because the temptation when you are going through a difficult time in your life is to not be a person you'd be proud to be. It's to act upon every emotional instinct that you have, the rage that you're feeling, the sadness, the betrayals, all of that. Try to set it aside and take the high road consistently. So it was a conscious thought, ringing in my head, literally, repeatedly, every day. Therefore, when the media would call, there was either no response or a very positive response." In addition to demonstrating an ability to identify his own emotions during a problematic event, this leader consciously took those negative emotions he was feeling and turned them into a positive reaction.

A school leader from the Midwest told us how he tries to apply this resilience strategy, "One of the things I recognize as the leader is that as I go emotionally, so goes the rest of my administrators and my district. I constantly remind myself that if I don't communicate a sense that things are going to get better and there is hope, then there is no one else to give them this message. So, I truly believe it's part of my essence as a leader and that it is a major responsibility of leadership." Identifying times of high emotion as a signal to use emotion to shape thought is a valuable tool to strengthen leader resilience.

After leaders successfully realize their emotions in tough times and how these emotions could affect performance, they must exercise caution to never take action before sufficiently gaining control of their own emotions. Carmen Grey, a central office administrator in Maine, mentioned using a positive outlook on life as a way controlling her own emotions and actions. "If I have a disappointment, I say, 'Okay,' I just need 30 minutes alone to show self pity.

From there I move on." The administrator described how she blew it one night by not putting the strategy into practice at a very difficult board meeting. "I did respond publicly when the board was totally out of control one night. Reacting emotionally and without thought I said, 'This board needs to learn some manners if you are going to get a new superintendent.' And because that board is notorious for acting badly, people in the audience were thrilled with my comments and I got a standing ovation. But I felt very badly about having said it, to have put the board in that position was not my intention."

As many leaders can attest, the momentarily satisfying emotional response may sabotage opportunity for a cooperative working relationship in the future. Resilient leaders stay in touch with their emotions during adversity and make sure they choose emotions that will have positive implications for their resilience capacity in the future.

SPIRITUAL WELL-BEING

In our work with leaders across the globe, we get a range of sentiments expressed about both the meaning and the role of spirituality in contributing to the resilience capacity of leaders. But whether leaders are atheist, agnostic or devoutly religious, we found two unifying threads woven among virtually all resilient leaders' belief systems. One is a belief in a cause beyond one's self; the other is a belief in a Universal strength greater than one's self. In almost all contexts, we discovered that spirituality is a sustaining lifeline for leaders in tough times.

Paul Houston and colleagues (Houston & Sokolow, 2006; Houston, Blankstein, & Cole, 2008) have written extensively on the subject of spirituality, religion, and leaders. In general they contend that spirituality is a broader term than religion. They offered this definition of spirituality, "spirituality is the energy that connects us to the deity. It is also the energy that connects us to each other and to our deepest selves" (2008, p. 8). Houston underscored his belief that the foundation of spirituality in leaders rests on the leader's desire to serve. The more that the leader's underlying intention is to benefit others, the more the leader will engender support from the Universe. (2006, p. 1). The authors added, "spirituality allows the leader to refill the well and to progress toward an uncertain future" (p. 10). As leaders grow stronger from the contribution that spirituality makes to renewal of their resilience capacity, they develop an even deeper sense of spirituality to tackle greater adversity that lies ahead.

Spirituality provides a way of thinking and acting that allows leaders' best selves to emerge. This thinking can contribute insights about how to engage leaders' internal spiritual compass during adversity. It can propel them to think beyond their own self-interest needs. Keeping the greater good as a focus provides stamina and fortitude to stay the course when the immediate leadership crisis appears insurmountable. Patterson and Kelleher (2005) reinforced this point, "school leaders must stay connected to their deepest values if they are to persist and withstand the adversity sure to come their way, and for many leaders, those deepest values spring from their spirituality" (p. 123)

Regardless of the specific interpretation of what spirituality means on a theoretical level, we found that it translates into a common language on a practical level. Leaders with a deep sense of spirituality transfer this sense to others. They help people find meaning and faith in their work. They also help people answer fundamental questions about themselves and their organizations: Who am I as an individual? Who are we as a people? What is the purpose of my life, or our collective life? What ethical principles should we follow? What legacy should we leave? Can we resolve conflict and rise above adversity to realize our mission? (Bolman & Deal, 2008).

As leaders confront these questions, they do so with eyes open to reality. They understand that there are times when their work as leaders will be exciting, uplifting, and enjoyable at its best, and relentless, frustrating, and exhausting at its worst. Through the highs and lows of the resilience cycle, spirituality is strengthened for leaders as they apply the following strategies to sustain them through all of these of times.

Action Strategy: Resilient Leaders Turn to Personal Reflection or Connections to a Higher Purpose in Life as a Source of Strength During Adversity

Many leaders find strength when they turn into themselves for reflection and contemplation. This does not mean they turn away from others. When chronic or crisis conditions erupt, leaders turn inward to refocus on their de raison d'être, their reason for being, as well as to follow their spiritual, moral compass for direction. Spiritual reflection can occur in a variety of contexts: a daily run through a neighborhood, a walk in the park, journal writing, time spent with family, or time alone for quiet contemplation.

Extended quiet time can also provide the base for spiritual renewal. Shalia Carrington, a middle school principal, got a surprise call due to reduction in force informing her she needed to move to an assistant principal's assignment in another school. Carrington confessed, "I didn't want to leave my school and under no circumstances did I want to go to the assigned school because of the reputation they had. But it was inevitable, so I dropped off my stuff in my new office and took a self-imposed three week sabbatical. When I returned I just hit the ground running. And it turned out to be a growing experience for me." When we asked Carrington what she reflected on during her unexpected sabbatical, she responded, "I thought about the reasons I didn't want to go. It was an extremely tough student body. Then I began to think what I could do to make them love school and leave the streets. Finally I just came to the conclusion that must be where God wanted me to be. There must be some child or children that I was supposed to be there for. I took the time away to gather the strength and state of mind to do it. I knew deep down that I could." And she did. Since that experience Carrington finished her doctorate and was promoted within the district.

Davidson and Dreher (2003) issued a cautionary warning that spirituality is not a panacea if one is suffering from emotional problems. But they argued, "My almost three decades of experience with anxiety patients has convinced me that integrating spirituality or the pursuit of meaning into the healing process can be of value, along with medical or psychological treatments and self-care skills" (p. 280). Incorporating spiritual renewal techniques may help the leader to step back as needed from the stress of the day-to-day pressing leadership business, to regain the inner strength and insights to successfully move forward.

Leon Figg, a Tennessee principal, found himself in a school district with a set of small, divided communities inhabited by artistic large city transplants on one side and a conservative rural population on the other. Challenging demographics were just the tip of the proverbial iceberg. Fiscal times were tough, enrollment was declining, and membership on the board of education was unstable. Leading during this time was challenging, felt dangerous, and required constant rebalancing. Figg, frequently feeling on the defensive and exhausted by all the turmoil, found it easier to do battle for short term results than apply long term strategies.

"For two years I found that the conflict involved in this situation threatened to ambush my ethics and core values. This created conflict within me as well as around me, exhausting my ability to make sound decisions. I began to question my ability to remain as superintendent in this district or even to lead effectively anywhere. But due to something in my fiber, I could not leave the job. That's when I took some time to reflect, and refocus on my entire life. I recognized that I was part of the problem. I was focusing most of my creative energy on my work instead of dispersing it to other areas of my life as well. This over-fixation with my job situation made my approach too intense for the dynamics of the district, and helped to keep the conflict level escalated."

Clearly, Figg turned inward to regain the inner strength and insights necessary to successfully move forward. He summarized his thoughts about inner reflection this way, "It does keep a smile on my face, strengthens my resolve, and helps me persist in the face of daunting circumstances, the daily work of school superintendents." This daily work in the form of long hours, short tempers, too many students, not enough space, under prepared and overtaxed staff, high expectations, and low funding adds to the complexity of leadership. It is easy to lose oneself in the maze of leadership responsibilities, or to bring only a part of oneself to the leadership table. A clear head and a renewed spirit can reduce the impact of stress and improve the effectiveness of one's leadership skills.

Leaders also turn outward and upward for spiritual strength. According to accounts shared with us by leaders, looking upward to the deity in the form of organized religion is the primary source of resilience in their lives. When we asked Renita Vega about her major source of strength as she struggled for ten years battling corrupt forces trying to take away her school, she reflected a few moments then commented about her faith as the primary source of strength during adversity, "We were taught from the time I was born that you trust God with your life and he has proven himself, once, twice, three times. We were taught to recognize God's hands." So when Vega found herself facing tremendous challenges, she told us, "I was able to look back and remember that God was faithful in getting us through this in the past. He will get us through this, too."

A school leader in the Southwest reinforced the importance of faith to him, "Religion is very important to me. It keeps me going every day. I meet monthly with a priest to discuss my work. I also meet with a pastor for prayer groups and I pray weekly with staff members. I feel very blessed in that way."

Not all leaders count among their blessings a sense of spirituality. Ben Himes, a Pupil Services Director in Montana, responded with a chuckle when asked about the role spirituality played in his decisions during adverse situations. He expressed doubt that his actions during adversity were ever very spiritual. He said that during times of difficulty he let his emotions guide his reactions. Throughout the conversation he maintained that he did not have a spiritual sense about things. Yet in conversations with his subordinates, it was clear that they saw him very differently than he saw himself. They described Ben as a man worth following because he is respectful and trusting. They added that he could be counted on to show compassion even to an adversary and to give hope in situations that seemed hopeless. Perhaps if Ben turned inward more he would discover the spirituality that others already have discovered.

Even though scholars may disagree on the primary sources of spirituality, most agree that a leader's spiritual roots lead to expanding enlightenment. According to Tolle (2005), the Universe demands that we pay attention to what can change our lives. He explained that as leaders we learn lessons in adversity and the reward for appreciating a first lesson is a second lesson. For Tolle, each lesson we experience becomes a stairway to the next lesson and movement toward enlightenment. In addition to the enlightenment leaders gain through their own lessons, they gain even more by helping others identify and work through their lessons. Enlightened leaders are aware of their intentions and naturally focus them on serving others even in the face of strong opposition.

Action Strategy: Resilient Leaders Feel a Deep Spiritual Gratitude for the Opportunity to Pursue a Calling of Leadership, Especially During Tough Times

Gratitude is generally acknowledged as a feeling of thankfulness and appreciation for something given to us, be it tangible or intangible. Personally, gratitude may be expressed for family and good health. Professionally, leaders may be grateful to others for extending the calling to lead. To channel their gratitude, leaders must *recognize intellectually* that which they value, *acknowledge willingly* that for which they are grateful, and *appreciate emotionally* the goodness they are given (Emmons, 2007, p. 5). Without gratitude, leaders cannot acknowledge those people, circumstances or events that enable them to lead effectively. In Emmons' words, "We could not be who we are or where we are in life without the contributions of others" (Emmons, 2007, p. 5).

The benefits of gratitude are substantial, personally and professionally. On the personal level, recent research (Emmons, 2007) asserts that when people systematically engage in cultivating an "attitude of gratitude," they experience a variety of measurable benefits, including psychological, physical, and interpersonal. Specifically, adults who kept gratitude journals on a regular basis exercise more frequently, report fewer illness symptoms, feel better about their lives as a whole, and are more optimistic about the future (p. 11) when compared with those who were asked to chronicle their daily troubles or to reflect on ways in which they were better off than others.

On a professional level, it is difficult to imagine how effective leaders function without regular recognition of gratitude for those with whom they work. Leader resilience is strengthened when leaders recognize that, even in the worst of times, goodness exists. This skill is part of the resilience thinking skills we examined in Chapter 2.

Leaders must recognize that there is a cycle to gratitude in which sometimes they are the recipient and, at other times, the giver of benefits. Not only do others contribute to leaders' well-being, but also, as givers, leaders recognize the needs of others and are able to support those needs. The cycle allows leaders to receive with gratitude and to pass on the benefits they receive to others. On the other hand, *in*gratitude results in a reduction, a constricting, lesser sense of self. We associate emotions such as anger, defensiveness, bitterness, and resentment with ingratitude and recognize the confinement leaders feel when bound by "ingratitude."

Developing the habit of gratitude is not an easy task. Even Albert Einstein struggled, "A hundred times a day I remind myself that my inner and outer life depends on the labors of other men, living and dead, and that I must exert myself in order to give in the full measure I have received and am still receiving." Emmons (2007) recommended several research-based strategies that leaders can use to increase gratitude.

1. Keep a gratitude journal. Remind yourself in writing of the many benefits you receive and the people who contribute to your life. Being grateful and acknowledging the specifics reminds us of the goodness in life. No need to worry about sentence structure, grammar or mechanical; writing your thoughts is the goal. Writing helps organize your thoughts and gives a way to reflect on your experiences.
2. Remember the bad. Writing about nastiness is one way to deal with it, to see it in a different light and gain a better understanding of where opportunities lie. If your gratitude list is redundant or weak, keep doing it and it will gain power as you begin to watch for benefits and contributions to your life. Further, writing about the bad things in life provides a way to reflect on those times, to consider what we did right that helped us through. Writing about gratitude builds our resilience as we reflect up on and nourish strategies that help us make it through tough times. Remembering where we used to be and seeing where we are now can be enlightening.
3. Ask yourself three questions. A Buddhist meditation technique involves asking yourself:

What have I received from _____?
What have I given to _____?
What troubles and difficulties have I caused _____?

The first question, of course, recognizes all the richness that leaders receive from others and heightens their gratitude. The second question focuses on what leaders give to others and, in so doing, reminds them of their connectedness to those in their lives. Many leaders find this a way of "giving back" that keeps them in touch with goodness. The last question is likely the most difficult to answer. In considering what trouble leaders cause others, they are acknowledging the potential for pain to others created by leadership words and actions. As leaders, this is an important part of checking reality, a concept we discussed in Chapter 2. This reflective question also calls upon leaders to acknowledge how they contributed to that reality, a concept we will examine in Chapter 10.

Leaders who take the time first to reflect on their beliefs about gratitude and then act consistent with their beliefs demonstrate spirituality and strengthen their resilience. Acts of resilience were expressed in many ways by the leaders we interviewed. Gratitude for personal support through tough times was a major theme, including appreciation for family, friends, networks, and God. We discussed specific examples in Chapter 5. For now we want to underscore a fundamental point about gratitude that we made in the beginning of this section. Sincere gratitude must include all of these elements: leaders must *recognize intellectually* that which they value, *acknowledge willingly* that for which they are grateful, and *appreciate emotionally* the goodness they are given, and then *convey this appreciation* to others who contributed to the sense of gratitude leaders feel.

To summarize this section, spirituality is liberating. It frees leaders' spirit to move beyond the intentions of self-interest to intentions of a cause beyond one's self. And, as Houston and Sokolow (2006) observed, the more leaders' underlying intention focuses on benefiting others, the more the leaders will engender support from the Universe. This in turn leads to a deepening of spirituality as an invaluable resource during tough times.

PHYSICAL WELL-BEING

Physical well-being is part of the organic relationship among the other ingredients of a leaders' well-being. The close positive relationship between overall personal well-being and physical well-being is irrefutable. Patterson and Kelleher (2005) underscored the importance of physical energy, "Physical energy is the underlying source of fuel for all dimensions of your performance. It affects your feelings of vitality and alertness, your ability to manage your emotions, and your mental sharpness, creativity, motivation, and commitment. The size of your energy reserves depends on what and how you eat, the amount you sleep, and your level of fitness" (p. 107).

Physical well-being is directly subject to the lifestyle leaders choose to live. Leaders who fail, in the long run, to take into account their physical well-being put at risk their leadership performance. It can happen easily. As Crowley and Lodge so forcefully stated, "The game has changed for us because we have luxuries and choices in our modern lives that have no parallel in our biology. In a remarkable triumph of ego over intellect, we simply assume that we were 'made' for this life; that we were purpose-built for life in the twenty-first century. That is a mistaken view and we must get over it. . . . our ancestors ran for their lives for hundreds of millions of years, desperately searching for food, storing it up in their bodies against the certainty of drought, ice and starvation. And then, in a twinkling that was all gone and a fundamental law of creation ceased to apply. This is arguably the most profound shift, ever, in the way the world works. . . . In short, we have adopted a life style which—for people designed as we were designed—is nothing less than a disease." The authors call for a more active physical life because that's how humans are genetically wired.

The research on living a healthy life is abundant and it is conclusive. Leaders know what to do. Then why is it so hard to do? The constant struggle for leaders is how to find the *time* to make it happen.

Action Strategy: Resilient Leaders Protect Time to renew their Emotional, Physical and Spiritual Well-Being

Never do we hear leaders say, "I have too much time on my hands." In leaders' personal and professional lives "not enough time to get it done" is a standard mantra. Jerry Patterson recalled when he struggled with finding time for personal health as superintendent, "I frequently complained that I did not have enough time to exercise on a regular basis, but the job demands prevented it. I made this comment in a meeting with other local superintendents, and a colleague superintendent mused that he found time to run four marathons the past year. Touché. We both had the same job description. I was no more conscientious or effective than he was as a superintendent. I had some soul-searching to do about how to protect time to tend to my physical well-being."

Resilient leaders find ways to make time, even though they can't manufacture more time. It is a matter of a well-researched theme called time management. Patterson and Kelleher (2005) stressed the importance of managing personal energy, "Managing your personal energy and holding yourself responsible for how you manage it are just as important as holding yourself responsible for managing other precious personal and organizational resources, such as money and time" (p. 111). While the activities that successfully accomplish this replenishment will be different from leader to leader, the commonality across effective leaders is that they consciously try to find a sense of balance in their lives.

In demanding leadership roles, a balanced life may not be possible if balance is defined strictly by time. Instead, a balanced life for leaders means striking a balance in remaining true to the values that matter most in the Personal Values Hierarchy described in Chapter 3. And it is easy to fall out of balance. As one school leader revealed his own personal struggles leading his district in the heat of a violent crisis (Patterson, Goens, & Reed, 2008), "Slowly and almost imperceptibly, I fell out of balance: emotionally, physically, cognitively, and spiritually. When needs in one or more of these areas are ignored, we get into trouble. That's what happened to me. Even if I knew it was happening at the time, I don't think I would admit it. Leaders after all, I thought, are supposed to be strong. But what is strength?" He added, "I never shared my feelings of fear of not being up to the task of handling the crisis. Feeling a deep sense of responsibility haunted me, even though rationally I knew an emotionally disturbed twenty-one year old with bizarre schemes in his head could not be stopped under almost any circumstance. My second-guessing produced doubts in my mind that maybe more might have been done."

Burying feelings and being an anchor amid chaos requires a countervailing balance. Care-taking and helping others does not mean leaders can deny their own grief and needs. Recognizing them, however, is one sign of strength. And then taking action to carve out the time to return to a sense of balance brings well-being into alignment.

A veteran leader we interviewed offered this advice to new leaders about how to use time to help restore balance:

- "Find solitude. Go somewhere quiet like a park or a lake and just sit, reflect and reenergize and center yourself.
- "Write your thoughts in a journal. Contemplate your feelings both current and past and see if you are growing in understanding of what gives you joy and what causes you sadness or discouragement.
- "Exercise not only your mind but your body and do it with friends.
- "Get professional help after a very serious crisis or talk to someone in stressful situations who will tell you what you need to hear even if it isn't what you want to hear."

Above all else leaders need to have the strength to come to terms with the reality that they are responsible for achieving a balance in their own well-being. Otherwise, in the long run they cannot lead responsibly

The principle of less is more applies to this strategy. Less work and more rest provides the formula for a higher rate of return to work. Rested leaders perform tasks with less effort and with greater energy. Research on sleep strongly suggests that we are operating on a false notion that we can do with less. Clearly, we can face adversity much more effectively rested. Sam Greene, Deputy Superintendent in a Virginia suburb said, "I find alone time for reflection because that helps to rejuvenate me. He continued, "The other thing I do which a lot of other superintendents don't do is I don't let myself get consumed with my job. I don't go in at 6:30 a.m. and work till 10:00 p.m. I certainly do my 60–70 hour weeks, but I don't let myself get consumed, because you know what, I'll never recapture that moment with one of my kids or a funny moment with the pug. You have to be jealous of that and you have to be protective of that."

Regular physical check-ups, trips to the dentist and eye doctor are nonnegotiable physical well-being requirements. Doctor-prescribed therapy regimens should be nonnegotiable. They cannot be disturbed by the work schedule. They simply must come first. Former superintendent Justin Franklin's story emphasized the importance of monitoring and attending to personal health factors, "Thirteen years ago I was experiencing unusual physical discomfort when I started my daily run. Fortunately, I was on a schedule of annual physical examinations. I raised concern about what I was experiencing in the conference with my long term physician, just after I had successfully completed a physical examination that included an electrocardiogram. After taking numerous tests prescribed by my physician that were inconclusive, a final test, an angiogram, revealed complete blockage in one artery and partial blockage in another. Fortunately, no heart damage was found during heart surgery which was completely successful." Justin reported that it was a life changing event. "In spite of my exercise regimen, I had failed to heed the clear indicators that I was allowing too much stress to enter my life. Divorce, relocation, board of education membership change, and child rearing issues combined to produce a depressed mental state that required medication." Now, thirteen years later, Justin was happy to report, "Since that wake-up call my health has been excellent. Due to my better ability to monitor my stress level I'm able to have an even better life style that still includes running and racquetball, but now includes a much improved diet."

Ken Oxford, an assistant principal in North Carolina, talked about a lesson he learned the hard way about the use of time for renewal, "I have a 45 minute commute home at the end of the work day. For years this time was spent reviewing the mistakes I made during the day." He lamented how he drove home each night with his mind filled "with should haves": "I *should* have waited to speak to the whole staff. I *should* have asked them to meet before they made any decisions, I *should* have known better than to trust that they would do the right thing, I *should* never have assumed they knew what to do." He said that by the time he arrived home each night, he was tense and exhausted. His final thought before sleep was often, "I should never have taken this job."

Upon reflection he realized that the long car ride home could have been an opportunity to recharge his battery listening to music or a book on tape, enjoying the scenery, or looking forward to relaxing activities awaiting him at home.

Adversity may be unavoidable and may come without warning at the very worst of times. When bad things happen, resilient leaders rely on their personal well-being as an energy source to give them strength to act on the courage of their convictions. By acting on the action strategies discussed in this chapter, emotional, spiritual, and physical well-being will be enriched.

SUMMARY

This chapter focused on the ESP of a leader's well-being. The emotional, spiritual, and physical well-being of leaders is crucial to their resilience. Even though we examined each element of well-being separately, we emphasized that the *wholeness* of well-being is greater than the total of the separate parts. Each element depends on the others to sufficiently fuel the resilience energy of leaders. We provided action strategies leaders can implement to improve their overall well-being and thereby boost their resilience to tackle larger issues in the future.

CHARTING YOUR RESILIENCE PROFILE
FOR PERSONAL WELL-BEING

To chart your Leader Resilience Profile for *Personal Well-Being* return to your completed LRP Survey in Chapter 1, then follow these steps:

- For each item number listed, circle your *actual* item response on the chart.
- Determine the *conversion* score for the item, located directly beneath the *actual* number you circled.
- Enter your conversion score in the box on the extreme right column of the chart.
- Sum the scores in the right column to determine your Resilience Strength Score for *Personal Well-Being*. **Note:** You will have three separate subscale scores for Personal Well-Being: *Emotional, Spiritual, and Physical.*
- Observe your individualized score for each subscale on the continuum from Moderately Low to Very High.

Table 6.1. Personal Well-Being Subscales

Strength: Emotional Well-Being

Item #	Item Response	Enter your Conversion Score for the Item
28	If your *actual* item response is: 1 2 3 4 5 6 Then your *conversion* score is: 6 5 4 3 2 1 **enter your conversion score in the box**	
34	If your *actual* item response is: 1 2 3 4 5 6 Then your *conversion* score is: 6 5 4 3 2 1 **enter your conversion score in the box**	
39	If your *actual* item response is: 1 2 3 4 5 6 Then your *conversion* score is: 1 2 3 4 5 6 **enter your conversion score in the box**	
45	If your *actual* item response is: 1 2 3 4 5 6 Then your *conversion* score is: 1 2 3 4 5 6 **enter your conversion score in the box**	
50	If your *actual* item response is: 1 2 3 4 5 6 Then your *conversion* score is: 6 5 4 3 2 1 **enter your conversion score in the box**	
55	If your *actual* item response is: 1 2 3 4 5 6 Then your *conversion* score is: 1 2 3 4 5 6 **enter your conversion score in the box**	
	Strength Score: Emotional Well-Being	

Strength Score Continuum for Emotional Well-Being

Resilience Level	Moderately Low	Moderate	Moderately High	Very High

Table 6.1.   Personal Well-Being Subscales

Strength: Spiritual Well-Being

Item #	Item Response	Enter your Conversion Score for the Item
16	If your *actual* item response is: 1 2 3 4 5 6 Then your *conversion* score is: 1 2 3 4 5 6 **enter your conversion score in the box**	
22	If your *actual* item response is: 1 2 3 4 5 6 Then your *conversion* score is: 6 5 4 3 2 1 **enter your conversion score in the box**	
29	If your *actual* item response is: 1 2 3 4 5 6 Then your *conversion* score is: 1 2 3 4 5 6 **enter your conversion score in the box**	
40	If your *actual* item response is: 1 2 3 4 5 6 Then your *conversion* score is: 6 5 4 3 2 1 **enter your conversion score in the box**	
35	If your *actual* item response is: 1 2 3 4 5 6 Then your *conversion* score is: 1 2 3 4 5 6 **enter your conversion score in the box**	
72	If your *actual* item response is: 1 2 3 4 5 6 Then your *conversion* score is: 1 2 3 4 5 6 **enter your conversion score in the box**	
	Strength Score: Spiritual Well-Being	

Strength Score Continuum for Spiritual Well-Being

Resilience Level	Moderately Low	Moderate	Moderately High	Very High

Table 6.1. Personal Well-Being Subscales

Strength: Physical Well-Being

Item #	Item Response							Enter your Conversion Score for the Item
10	If your *actual* item response is:	1	2	3	4	5	6	
	Then your *conversion* score is:	1	2	3	4	5	6	
	enter your conversion score in the box →							
71	If your *actual* item response is:	1	2	3	4	5	6	
	Then your *conversion* score is:	6	5	4	3	2	1	
	enter your conversion score in the box →							
60	If your *actual* item response is:	1	2	3	4	5	6	
	Then your *conversion* score is:	6	5	4	3	2	1	
	enter your conversion score in the box →							
65	If your *actual* item response is:	1	2	3	4	5	6	
	Then your *conversion* score is:	1	2	3	4	5	6	
	enter your conversion score in the box →							
4	If your *actual* item response is:	1	2	3	4	5	6	
	Then your *conversion* score is:	1	2	3	4	5	6	
	enter your conversion score in the box →							
59	If your *actual* item response is:	1	2	3	4	5	6	
	Then your *conversion* score is:	1	2	3	4	5	6	
	enter your conversion score in the box →							
	Strength Score: Physical Well-Being →							

Strength Score Continuum for Physical Well-Being

Resilience Level →	Moderately Low	Moderate	Moderately High	Very High
Score Range →	13–18	19–24	25–30	31–36

Part IV

Resilience Action Skills

Chapter 7

Resilient Leaders Persevere

Resilient leaders may seem like ordinary leaders in ordinary times. But these are turbulent times. Today we need extraordinary leaders who find the strength to persevere and endure in spite of overwhelming obstacles. Extraordinary leaders do not have to be decorated hero leaders. Most resilient leaders are everyday people who reflect the mosaic of diversity across the globe. One strength found among all of these leaders is the demonstrated ability to persevere and grow stronger through ongoing adversity. In this chapter we focus initially on what persevering looks like and how it differs from its cousins, such as prevailing. Then we examine specific strategies leaders can apply to help them persevere and even thrive in the midst of all of the apparent chaos.

WHAT IS LEADER PERSEVERANCE?

To answer this question, we first need to distinguish between the acts of a leader prevailing, a leader persisting, and a leader persevering.

Leaders prevail when they demonstrate dominance or strength in their influence over others or when they doggedly gain the upper hand. In other words, they conquer. If they conquer adversity, that have persevered in a positive sense. If they conquer others, they have persevered in a negative way. So even though leaders may prevail and live to fight another day, this is not what we mean by leader perseverance.

Sometimes perseverance is described as synonymous to persistence. But in fact that is missing a fundamental point. Persistence means refusing to give up at all costs. Leaders can demonstrate persistence when they obstinately, stubbornly pursue a course of action at the expense of others or without regard for their own integrity as a leader. A superintendent may "dig in her heels" and persist in getting her way with the board on a pet agenda of hers, even if it costs her credibility with the board in the long run. In summary, persistence is a necessary but not sufficient condition for perseverance.

Also leaders may be motivated to persist in achieving outcomes because of the consequences of not achieving them. School leaders may persist in implementing school board or state department of education mandates out of fear or concern for the impact on them if they fail to comply. But we contend that leaders in these circumstances are not demonstrating perseverance.

In our view leaders demonstrate perseverance in the face of adversity when they voluntarily and relentlessly pursue a course of action, consistent with their core values about what matters most, and without regard for discouragement, barriers, or previous failure—unless it is absolutely clear all realistic strategies have been exhausted.

THE BENEFITS OF PERSEVERANCE

The preponderance of research points to many benefits attributed to perseverance. Not surprisingly, leaders who persevere significantly increase their odds of achieving difficult goals that are complicated by adverse circumstances. It is a rare leadership setting where leaders continuously undertake major initiatives and are greeted by a steady stream of successes and positive feedback. As discussed throughout this book, adversity is inevitable, but resilience is optional. Leaders who don't give up when adversity strikes, who relentlessly pursue goals they are passionate about, these are the leaders who receive intrinsic rewards for their persistence. Research shows that leaders appreciate their accomplishments more when they have had to endure considerable difficulty in achieving them.

In addition to the reward of current accomplishment, successful perseverance now becomes a strong motivator and confidence-builder to tackle more formidable adversity in the future. Leaders who persevere must develop new approaches and skill sets that can be beneficial in subsequent undertakings. And self-efficacy gets a boost when leaders achieve "hard-fought" victories over adversity.

ACTION STRATEGIES TO STRENGTHEN PERSEVERANCE

So far in this chapter, we have discussed what leader perseverance is (and what it is *not*), and we have briefly summarized the benefits of leader perseverance. Now we turn our attention to the action strategies to strengthen leader resilience in the area of perseverance.

Action Strategy: Resilient Leaders Maintain a Steady, Concentrated Focus on the most Important Priorities until Success is Attained

Leaders became leaders, in part, because they demonstrated the ability to be intense in their pursuit of goals. Resilient leaders distinguish themselves from not-so-resilient leaders in those circumstances when adversity erects major roadblocks along the road to success. Resilient leaders call upon several strengths to help them maintain a long-term focus on attaining success.

First, resilient leaders act on their belief that they can have a strong measure of control over what happens to them when adversity strikes. Psychologists refer to this as a leader's internal locus of control. In its most basic form, "I am in charge of producing successful outcomes when the odds are stacked against me." This core belief empowers leaders to take risks even though they know they may likely encounter short term setbacks. Despite the temporary defeat, resilient leaders have confidence that they can overcome the setbacks in the long run. A belief in themselves gives them strength to stay the course through a steady, concentrated focus.

In our work with urban school principals, we noticed a discernible difference in how principals think about their position. Those who are most successful are those who stay focused, for several years, building a school culture of high performance. When an elementary school principal was asked recently if he was ready to take on additional challenges as a middle school principal, he said rather proudly, "I made a commitment to make a difference in the lives of these students. I am the right person for the job and I am not finished here yet. New challenges will still be waiting for me when the time comes." The research on effective superintendents in urban settings revealed similar results. They demonstrate the strength to stay the course, in the face of chronic obstacles and temptations for advancement.

Also, an internal sense of control means that resilient leaders take seriously the obligation to stay focused. Instead of waiting for others to assign actions to be taken, resilient leaders take personal responsibility for their own actions. According to Peterson and Seligman (2004) this makes the task chosen more relevant to "self." Plus, leaders with a strong sense of internal control look for ways they contributed to the bad situation or their initial failures in trying to overcome the bad situation. Less resilient leaders who operate from an external sense of control blame external forces for their setbacks and their failed attempts to overcome setbacks to external forces. These dynamics make it more difficult to sustain a concentrated focus and to find the energy to bounce back from adverse circumstances. Some leaders self-declare their mission as change agents. They ride into town, move organizational chart boxes around, implement personally mandated reforms, and, when the heat gets too intense, they ride out of town, blaming others for the lack of systemic success.

A large body of literature points to the fact that less resilient leaders erect barriers (self handicapping) to get in the way of their own success. If they fail they can blame it on the barriers. Erecting barriers is a clear signal that these leaders don't have a strong commitment to the outcomes. Their commitment is to the preservation of self-image when their leadership strategies fail to overcome the barriers. An example is the principal who told us, "I took this job knowing all the time that it was a no-win situation. It's been three years, I have not won a major battle yet, but I am leaving the district with added experience to help me in the future." If by chance the self-handicapping leaders do succeed, then they can take credit for success in spite of the barriers, barriers they actually erected in the first place.

Another strategy less resilient leaders employ is to avoid taking any actions in tough circumstances until told what to do. Then if they fail in their attempted accomplishment, they can rationalize that they weren't able to control the actions they were assigned and, therefore, have no accountability for the failure. All of these strategies undercut the ability to stay focused in a concentrated way until success is achieved.

Resilient leaders conserve their energy in times of crisis because they distinguish between the issues that are most important and those issues, however large in scope, that are tangential to their overall mission and goals. Even though leaders may see that they can successfully overcome a wide range of difficult issues, they don't persist in attempting to overcome them all. Instead they concentrate their efforts on those issues that matter most to them. In this way they have more resilience capacity to stay focused. They do not dilute their energy by simultaneously taking on all challenges at the same time and with the same intensity.

Another ingredient that distinguishes resilient leaders is their drive toward high achievement. It comes as no surprise that some leaders are more driven to master the challenges that confront them. Sometimes this drive is fueled by the fear of failure and its impact on their self esteem. Resilient leaders don't tend to be driven by the fear factor. They are driven by their passionate commitment to do the best they can, especially in stressful circumstances. They thrive on the challenges posed by adversity. Instead of worrying about their self esteem if they fail, resilient leaders are motivated by their high self esteem and draw upon this belief in themselves to propel them through adversity. They refuse to be deterred by the prospects of failure. As we discuss later in the chapter, we don't advocate a leadership strategy of being driven to achieve at all costs. The Type A coronary-prone trait has been linked to persistence at all costs (Peterson & Seligman, 2004). Resilient leaders follow Kenny Rodger's advice of knowing when to hold them, when to fold them, when to walk away, and when to run.

Resilient leaders also find ways to make the tasks they must undertake interesting and appealing. Because they enjoy the immediate tasks, they can maintain a more concentrated focus on unpleasant issues. In other words, they don't have to enjoy the adversity *per se* to persevere but they need to some-how find enjoyment in the efforts they exert to overcome the adversity. We address in more depth this notion of resilience and joy in the article, "Joy and Resilience: Strange Bedfellows" (Patterson, Goens, & Reed, 2008).

Most leaders can see the complex of barriers that stand in their way toward moving beyond adversity to success. They understandably feel overwhelmed by what will be demanded of them to get there and they can't help wondering, "How can I possibly maintain a concentrated, steady focus on this unexpected adversity when I have so many other things going on in my life right now?" Resilient leaders demonstrate their ability to break down the tasks into man-ageable chunks. So when they stumble and fail to achieve a task along the way, they can adapt or regroup their efforts around a specific task rather than being overwhelmed by the enormity of all of the possible stumbling blocks ahead of them. Failure is not so discouraging if the failure is related to a task and not the entire project.

So resilient leaders learn to increase their concentration and focus when they channel their energy on the immediate task at hand, find ways to make the task more enjoyable, and know that failure on the initial efforts does not have to equate to failure on overcoming the big picture of adversity.

Action Strategy: Resilient Leaders never let Disruptive Forces and other Distractions Interfere with the Leadership Focus on Important Goals and Tasks

This strategy is a close cousin to the one we just discussed. The previous resilience strategy emphasizes a long term perspective on concentration. Resilient leaders apply another set of steps to stay focused in the short term. They avoid external disruptive forces and they monitor their own internal temptations to become distracted and lose focus.

One external force consists of oppositional groups that thrive on taking leaders away from their proverbial game plans for success. Many times these groups create the adversity in the first place. They officially organize with the singular purpose of prevailing on a specific issue, such as defeat of a school district referendum. Then they strategically plot to create turmoil in the life of school leaders. These self-interest groups know, from prior personal experience as well as the experience of others in the trenches, that any distraction in focus by leaders translates into more focused energy spent by the opposing forces as they relentlessly fight to win. As a veteran, ornery teacher union leader announced to the new superintendent his first week in the district, "Dr. Madison, there's one thing you might as well get clear in your head right now. I was here before you came and I will be here long after you are gone. And my sole mission is to get the biggest raise possible for the teachers, using whatever strategies it takes. That includes discrediting you if you get in the way."

The teacher union leader succeeded on all counts. He managed to divert the focus of the superintendent to reconciling teacher grievances and lawsuits, leaving little time for the district leader to build support around instructional values he held. He lasted three years. The teacher union leader is still there, having weathered five superintendents.

Resilient leaders craft several strategies to help them overcome these forces. As we have stated many times in this book, above all else resilient leaders are clear about what matters most. With this clarity of mind and purpose, leaders build in *system* safeguards that flag situations where the disruptive forces are mounting a counter attack. For example, as part of an ongoing strategic planning process, school leaders typically conduct environmental scans, constantly monitoring conditions in the community, the state, as well as nationally, that could prove to be distractions to the mission and vision of the organization. As part of the scan, the organization systematically engages in frameworks such as the SWOT model. Data are collected regarding Strengths, Weaknesses, Opportunities, and Threats that could affect the organization's plans. Leaders depend on these safeguards because they realize that they can't afford to consume a lot of their personal energy focusing on possible distractions. The leaders need structure built into the system committed to the cause of keeping the system energy focused during tough times.

Leaders also need *professional support* safeguards. As leaders regularly encounter adversity, both large and small, there is a tendency to fall into the pattern of treating all adversity as a crisis. To help counteract these tendencies and to improve focus on what matters most, savvy leaders rely on people close to them as their eyes and ears. Professional support comes in a variety of forms, including trusted colleagues within the system and valued mentors and other leaders in like positions outside the system. Individuals serving in these roles share an explicit understanding with the resilient leader that they are responsible for the human side of environmental scans looking for possible detractors to take the organization and the leader away from its intended mission.

Personal support is equally crucial to leaders successfully implementing this resilience strategy. We discussed the values of a support base at a broader level in Chapter 5. Now we are zeroing in on support of family and friends who serve the watchdog role of detecting patterns of the leader engaging in *behavioral drift*. By this we mean that leaders sometimes let distractions cause them to engage in actions that are not productive to their cause. As we described in Chapter 3, the alignment between actions and values is crucial to leaders' well-being. It is also crucial to their perseverance. For instance behavioral drift could show up in the form of a pattern of several nightly cocktails to clear the mind of adversity. Or it could be a pattern of channel surfing in the evening, searching for any negative news coverage about how the leader is failing to provide leadership in the face of chronic or crisis adversity.

Behavioral drift happens to all of us. It is not a sign of poor leadership or weakness when drift happens. It *is* a sign of resilient leadership when leaders recognize that they need to have personal support systems in place to help detect when this occurs, and give them candid, authentic feedback about it in the early stage of drifting. Finally, resilient leaders don't view such comments from their supporters as criticism or a sign of weakness. They value any signals that they are being unnecessarily distracted from their leadership focus.

In addition to external forces that try to take leaders away from their game plan, leaders must be cognizant of internal forces that operate to achieve the same outcome. A major internal factor that dilutes leaders' focus is self-imposed procrastination. We need to acknowledge, though, everyone procrastinates and many times for very good reasons. We are referring to a *pattern* of procrastination that impedes the ability to succeed in the face of adversity.

The most resilient leaders sustain resilient actions in tough times for positive reasons. They value their own success, a personal pride that comes from overcoming bad situations. They also value honoring their commitment to themselves and others to follow through on their intended actions even when the going gets tough. Finally resilient leaders persist, even after initial setbacks, because they have a strong belief in themselves. They know they possess the competence and confidence to clear whatever obstacles life erects.

Less resilient leaders tend to procrastinate for a variety of reasons. Some allow themselves to become distracted because the distracting activities are more immediately pleasing than the arduous tasks involved in figuring out how to persevere when the situation looks bleak. Chronic procrastinators also rationalize that they are being productive in their actions; it just doesn't happen to be actions that align with those needed to persevere through adversity. They have something to show for their efforts, so they aren't *wasting* time. In reality, though, they are wasting the opportunity. Their actions translate into misspent effort that doesn't advance the cause of success in tough times.

In a longitudinal study of procrastination, performance, stress, and health, Tice and Baumeister (1997) found that generally procrastination leads to stress, illness, and inferior performance. In other words procrastinators realize short term gains but encounter long term costs when they engage in such *distraction actions*. Not surprisingly, part of the appeal for procrastinators is to believe that these *distraction actions* confer genuine benefits to them. Indeed, benefits accrue until externally imposed deadlines force them to get to work or else risk the adverse effects of failure. And some leaders end up choosing failure rather than taking responsibility for their actions. They can always blame their poor performance on the forces they can't control. In summary, procrastinators end up suffering more and performing worse than resilient leaders who truly practice the mantra, "no pain, no gain. Let's just do it."

A major disruptive force that leaders encounter as they contemplate how to tackle adversity is the prospect of failure. This risk of failing is real and it becomes even more significant if the consequences of the failure carry significant loss to leaders' sense of personal efficacy. According to Peterson and Seligman (2004), "People are generally reluctant to lose or even risk losing some of their self-esteem and so whether they persist at a task or give up and withdraw may depend on what course of actions holds less threat of esteem loss" (p. 231). In other words the typical response to a fear of failure is to select the path that poses less threat to self-esteem or efficacy.

Resilient leaders approach this threat with a different framework for thinking about it. As we underscored in the chapters on resilience capacity, resilient leaders have a strong sense of self-efficacy. In the face of possible failure resilience calls for this type of thinking, "I acknowledge the magnitude of the threat and the difficulty I face in trying to overcome it. I also know that the very real possibility of possible outcomes will help me lead the organization closer to our goals. I stand firmly on the belief that there is no personal disgrace in my failing at difficult tasks. I believe in learning from the failure and moving on."

In a related way, resilient leaders avoid distraction in the form of assorted minor threats that pose possible hurdles to clear on the way to positive outcomes. If leaders spend scarce resilience energy on every conceivable threat to success, the resilience capacity shrinks, leaving inadequate energy to invest in overcoming the major league threats. When confronted with a bunch of minor threats posed by a parent self-interest group in one school, the school principal responded, "I am not even going to go there. We have too many other serious issues to confront and their petty points will be history by the end of the week." This is a clear example of refusing to let disruptive forces interfere with a leadership focus on the important goals and tasks.

Action Strategy: Resilient Leaders become more Persevering than ever when Confronted with the Next Round of Adversity

A point we made earlier is worth stating again. Leaders, particularly those early in their leadership career, tend to confront adversity with *if only* thinking. If only the school board would put students first, I could move ahead on what's important. If only I didn't have a contentious union, I could move ahead on terminating incompetent teachers.

We don't argue that the response pattern just described is bad judgment. To the contrary, we believe that it is natural. *Naturally* leaders (as well as others) want to believe that things will be o.k., even return to normal, when they get through the bad times. With more experience, leaders come to terms with the reality that adversity is inevitable. They recalibrate reality, shift their thinking from *if only* to *given the reality* thinking (described in detail in Chapter 2), and then focus their efforts on successful outcomes in spite of the adversity.

For some leaders, the bumps and bruises accumulated in trying to clear obstacles in the way take a toll on their resilience. They often conclude that it is not worth the effort it is going to require to tackle other chronic or crisis adversity when it inevitably surfaces again. Leaders who get discouraged by the recurring frustration and even pain of leadership in tough times lapse into what we referred to in Chapter 2 as realistic pessimists. They see the reality and difficulties that await them and decide it is not worth the human toll to take on the commitment to persevere.

Resilient leaders are realistic optimists. They too see the reality and the challenges that lie ahead. They however believe it is worth the effort to try to make a difference in achieving goals. But they reflect on what they have learned from their bouts with adversity—about what worked and didn't work. And they build on what they learned to help them become more persevering next time.

Most importantly, resilient leaders don't let earlier knock-downs and defeats affect their self efficacy. Research showed leaders who experienced initial failure and rebounded to become more resilient than ever in the face of new storms. The biggest gains in perseverance were marked by individuals who had high self-efficacy and high expectations they would successfully overcome the obstacles. Some people might label this as stubbornness. Resilient leaders would call themselves determined. They stay the course because they believe they can achieve success. They also look at the time, energy, and other resources they have invested in their confrontation with previous adversity and conclude, "I have too much invested to give up now in attaining what matters most."

In fact research shows that leaders with a history of intrinsic reward for their laborious efforts are more likely to exert greater effort in the future than leaders with a history of reward for low-effort leadership behavior. We want to emphasize here that there is a significant difference in the impact on future perseverance when rewards for success are externally versus internally driven. Researchers have concluded that people aren't motivated, in the long run, by external rewards for persistence. They found that when the reward is removed, performance drops off. If, however, the reward is structured to enhance self efficacy thereby enhancing the task's internal, symbolic value to the leader, then this intrinsic motivation leads to sustained perseverance.

Action Strategy: Resilient Leaders do not Let Adversity in One Aspect of their Life have a Long-term Impact on Resilience in Other Parts of their Life

A shorter version of this strategy is, "Compartmentalize." Find ways to protect the many dimensions of self from being diminished by adversity in one compartment of your life. A good model for leaders to learn from are the students in the school, particularly in urban settings, who come to school each day from a life after school that would test any person's resilience. An urban middle school principal we visited said, "I am extremely proud of the fact that the kids maintain such enthusiasm about learning, given some of their home environments. But they just don't bring the baggage from home into the school. In fact they are so protective and proud of the school, they don't let the bad apples come onto the school grounds."

We are not naïvely implying that leaders can build walls around each compartment to avoid spillover or contamination when bad things invade one dimension of self. For example, when a leader experiences the agony and stress resulting from being caretaker for elderly parents, in the short run spillover is unavoidable. The adverse conditions begin to drain a leader's physical and emotional well being.

When this happens, resilient leaders once again shift their thinking from *if only* thinking to *how can I* thinking. The internal dialog of a resilient leader may sound something like this: "My natural tendency is to want the adversity and pain suffered by my parent to go away. Then I could focus my resilience energy at work on overcoming the adversities waiting for me there. But the predicament is real and it is not going to go away. So I have to figure out how I can devote my resilience energy at home to being a quality caretaker and, at the same time, to persevere in doing my job well at work." Every leader acknowledges that the difficulties at home will have a direct impact at work, especially in the short run. In the long run, though, resilient leaders search for ways to replenish their energy so they can continue to be effective leaders without sacrificing their commitment to family. Clearly, under extreme sustained conditions, it may not be physically or emotionally possible to compartmentalize the stress. When these circumstances do occur, leaders are faced with preserving their overall health, even if it means downsizing or suspending their leadership responsibilities. As we elaborate in the next section, this is not the mark of defeat. It is a mark of resilience.

Resilient leaders also find ways to keep the long term stress of adversity in the work place in its place. When they are home, they avoid, to the extent possible, extensive conversations about the crisis at work. They resist the temptation to read community members' nasty blogs, media editorials, letters to the editor, and anonymous emails that question the leader's competence, ethics, and more. Although we are not recommending that leaders avoid any discussion with family about office issues, we do recognize that the leader role carries with it a certain amount of silent suffering. Not as martyr. Not as victim. But as a leader who is also a family member and cares deeply about protecting the family from unnecessary pain. Although it may sound somewhat contradictory, resilient leaders gain resilience strength when they realize they can absorb the angst of adversity and continue to be effective in their job while, at the same time, serve as buffer from family members experiencing the same level of angst.

Action Strategy: Resilient Leaders Persistently Refuse to give up, unless it is *Absolutely Clear* that all Realistic Strategies have been Exhausted

We have devoted the vast majority of this chapter to the first part of this strategy, not giving up. This section focuses on the second part, strengthening overall resilience by giving up on a goal when all realistic strategies have been exhausted. As we developed the Leader Resilience Profile (LRP), we found that our panel of experts providing feedback on the instrument items was split in their opinions about whether to drop the phrase "unless all realistic options have been exhausted." A significant number of reviewers felt that it was a sign of weakness, not resilience, to *ever* consider quitting. They held to the traditional leadership mantra, "Leaders never quit and quitters never win (or, in this book, persevere)." Even though we recognize the potential stigma of being labeled a loser or quitter, we choose to leave the second half of the strategy intact for several reasons.

Foremost, the belief that leaders should persevere at all costs ignores the reality that most of the time persevering through any chronic or crisis adversity includes the consequences of tough trade-off decisions and sacrifices by the leader. So from a philosophical as well as practical perspective the challenge is not, "persevere or otherwise be defeated." The overarching challenge is to determine to what extent other, more important values are compromised by the leader's perseverance on the specific issue of the moment. Several school leaders cited examples where, as one leader put it, "I gave it my best shot. But I could not continue to work under the blatantly unethical expectations demanded of me by the superintendent. It cost me big-time in terms of salary to leave. But I can still look at myself in the mirror each morning. That keeps me rich."

Carver and Scheier (2003) emphasized the difference between giving up effort and giving up commitment to the larger goal. The researchers framed their argument in terms of the principle of "hierarchicality among the goal values of the self." (p. 90). The authors elaborated:

"We believe that goals provide the structure that defines people's lives. The goals of the self take a variety of forms. Some are concrete (e.g., taking out the garbage): others are more abstract and ephemeral (e.g., being a good parent). What makes one goal matter more than another? Generally speaking, the higher in the hierarchy a goal is, the more important it is (the more central to the overall self). Concrete action goals acquire importance from the fact that attaining them serves the attainment of more abstract goals. The stronger the link between a concrete goal and the deepest values of the self, the more important is that concrete goal (p. 90)"

Patterson's research on the superintendency documented this predicament of choosing between competing core values. As he described in *The Anguish of Leadership* (Patterson, 2000), some of the superintendents gave up the goal of being a successful superintendent, and shifted their career path. Such disengagement from goals was deliberately chosen in the spirit of achieving a higher order personal goal of strengthening the core of personal efficacy we described in Chapter 4. Wise choices within this category of giving up develop over time into a resilience strength. We should emphasize, however, that the ability to make wise choices depends heavily on an individual's ability to be very clear about the hierarchy of personal values most important to defining self. The litmus test question becomes, "When confronted with the discouragement of likely failure, will giving up or continuing to fail represent the greatest risk to the hierarchy of values about what matters most to me?"

Research has shown that the consequences of ill-advised persistence are often more negative than the consequences of giving up. Thus the key to resilience is not in persistence at all costs, but persistence with a clear sense of one's hierarchy of value. When leaders do decide to give up on a goal, they need to be equally clear on the *why* behind the decision to quit. Jerry Patterson recalls sage advice he received from his colleague and supervisor when Jerry was in his 20s. Maury Sullivan advised him, "Jerry, as you make tough career decisions, make sure you are going *to* something, rather than *away* from something. Because if the answer to *why* is I want to run away from things without something more important you are running to, you may likely regret your decisions." Resilient leaders give up on a goal (career or personal) only if they come to this realization: if I continue to relentlessly pursue the goal, I will end up sacrificing higher order goals in the process of getting there.

SUMMARY

Leaders demonstrate perseverance in the face of adversity when they relentlessly pursue worthy goals, without being derailed by discouragement or barriers, until success is attained. Perseverance is a critical variable that distinguished between leaders who are effective in so-called normal times and leaders move through adversity with increased resilience to show for it. We documented strategies that resilient leaders put into practice so they won't fail under trying times.

CHARTING YOUR RESILIENCE PROFILE
FOR PERSEVERANCE

To chart your Leader Resilience Profile for *Perseverance,* return to your completed LRP Survey in Chapter 1, then follow these steps:

- For each item number listed, circle your *actual* item response on the chart.
- Determine the *conversion* score for the item, located directly beneath the *actual* number you circled.
- Enter your conversion score in the box on the extreme left of the chart.
- Sum the scores in the left column to determine your Resilience Strength Score for *Perseverance.*
- Observe your individualized score on the continuum from Moderately Low to Very High.

Table 7.1. Perseverance Subscale

Strength: Perseverance

Item #	Item Response	Enter your Conversion Score for the Item
33	If your *actual* item response is: 1 2 3 4 5 6 Then your *conversion* score is: 1 2 3 4 5 6 **enter your conversion score in the box →**	
38	If your *actual* item response is: 1 2 3 4 5 6 Then your *conversion* score is: 6 5 4 3 2 1 **enter your conversion score in the box →**	
44	If your *actual* item response is: 1 2 3 4 5 6 Then your *conversion* score is: 6 5 4 3 2 1 **enter your conversion score in the box →**	
49	If your *actual* item response is: 1 2 3 4 5 6 Then your *conversion* score is: 1 2 3 4 5 6 **enter your conversion score in the box →**	
54	If your *actual* item response is: 1 2 3 4 5 6 Then your *conversion* score is: 6 5 4 3 2 1 **enter your conversion score in the box →**	
69	If your *actual* item response is: 1 2 3 4 5 6 Then your *conversion* score is: 6 5 4 3 2 1 **enter your conversion score in the box →**	
	Strength Score: Perseverance →	

Strength Score Continuum for Perseverance

Resilience Level →	Moderately Low	Moderate	Moderately High	Very High
Score Range →	13–18	19–24	25–30	31–36

Chapter 8

Resilient Leaders are an Adaptive Species

It's not the strongest of the species, nor the most intelligent, that survives; it's the one most responsive to change.

—Charles Darwin

Darwin's words take on special meaning when tailored to life in today's organizations that struggle to survive. It's not the mightiest of organizations, nor the most intellectual, that thrive; it's those most responsive to change. When a complex social system like a school district faces difficult challenges, the organization needs evolutionary, and in some cases revolutionary, thinking and actions by leaders to thrive.

Typically in periods of disequilibrium, people scramble to restore stability by relying on established administrative processes. But applying staid management techniques to what Heifetz (1994) calls *adaptive* problems may prove to be futile. Today's turbulent times call for leadership that *disturbs* equilibrium. This is called *adaptive leadership.* In this chapter we examine adaptive leadership in times of uncertainty and ambiguity. First we respond to the question, "What is adaptive leadership?" We follow up this discussion with concrete strategies that resilient leaders can apply to strengthen their adaptive leadership skills.

HOW DO YOU KNOW ONE WHEN YOU SEE ONE?

What is adaptive leadership? "How do you know adaptive leaders when you see them?" A key to spotting adaptive leaders is by how they *think* and what they *do.* In short, adaptive leaders:

119

- See the world with fresh eyes. When the environment shifts around them, they adapt to changes through a network of relationships and feedback.
- Communicate throughout the organization the urgency and necessity for resilience and adaptability in the face of change.
- Establish broad and deep understanding of the circumstances that created the predicament and clarify why traditional solutions will not work. Leaders use the disequilibrium to move the system forward and change.
- Strive to hold organizational stressors at bay, so people are not overwhelmed, until solutions are defined. They work with others to confront the problems and pressure, but regulate, to the degree possible, the stress so that things do not break down and collapse into total dysfunction.
- Focus everyone's attention on results. Old approaches and processes applied to a dynamically changing context can be a recipe for failure. Leaders expand and open the boundaries of ideas and approaches and raise the ability for everyone to use their creativity to meet adversity productively.
- Understand the importance of refreshing and renewing themselves and the others working with them. Excelling in turbulent times is demanding and taxing, requiring courage and persistence on the part of everyone. Adaptive leaders are cognizant of the impact of ambiguity and stress on people's perspective and confidence.
- Identify and understand the driving forces affecting the organization. At times leaders need to create disequilibrium within the organization for it to address the transforming environment. Change may actually be easier to accept in uncertain times because perceivable threats are clearer. Discomfort and the danger of failure help people see focus on the importance of addressing problems and doing things differently.
- Use their intuitive sense to identify opportunities and undercurrents, and act decisively. People learn in many ways. Intuition is simply defined as having deep logical and conceptual knowledge about your job. It also involves the intangible and instinctive understandings gained from experience.

Leading is not easy. There is no script of certainty in life. Life does not always support a "heroic" leader who jumps into the breach against all odds and saves the day. Adaptive leaders, however, ensure that the organization learns to change, deals with ambiguity, and survives under pressure without being frozen and dependent on top-down direction. Leaders are expendable and total reliance on them to pull the chestnuts out of the fire by themselves is not realistic or desirable. Dependence is an anathema to adaptive resilience.

Leaders, however, are expected to be up to the challenges. But why do leaders fail to adapt and fall short? Heifetz (1994, p.36) identifies three main reasons. First, they may fail to perceive the nature of the threat in the environment. Leaders can only respond to the conditions they perceive. Second, they may recognize the threat, but the challenge may be beyond the organization's capability to respond adaptively. Finally, because of the distress caused by uncertainty and changes in the context, leaders may resist the pain, anxiety, and conflict associated with adapting and changing. They see the situation as overwhelming and too punishing. Nonadaptive leaders blame others, become distracted to other issues, jump to conclusions, or create an external enemy they can fault.

Another reason for failure to adapt is concern about acceptance. Adaptive leaders are not always accepted well and, in some cases, may be met with criticism and resistance. One of the great risks of leadership is challenging the organization out of its comfort zone because significant discomfort creates discord and turmoil. If leaders are attached to being popular, loved, and accepted, they often will not make the decision that creates the anxiety and productive discomfort that come with change.

Above all else, adaptive leaders have integrity. They know what they stand for, possess a strong moral compass, and act on the courage of their convictions. Turbulent times require a strong spine—core principles and values—that guides leaders in adverse times. Adaptable leaders are not "wishy-washy" about ethics. To the contrary, they are tight around values but flexible around the means to realize and implement them.

STRATEGIES TO STRENGTHEN ADAPTABLE LEADERSHIP

It's one thing to issue a challenge for leaders to be flexible when the going gets rough, but it's quite a different challenge to offer specific ideas about how to make it happen. We are up to the challenge. In this section we provide leaders with practical suggestions, supported by examples from colleague leaders.

Action Strategy: Resilient Leaders use Ongoing Feedback about the Reality of what's Happening and Possible in the Future and make Adjustments in Leadership Strategies

A Midwestern superintendent, Luke Bower, put the key into the ignition of his car and sat in the driveway watching the snowfall on a cold February day. He realized that things had shifted in the school district and the time to act on a $6 million technology plan for the schools was right. He and his staff had planned to present this proposal six months later in August.

He drove directly to the office, called his administrative team together, and said, "I've been thinking about this and I came to the conclusion that we should present a technology plan in the next 45 days. I know we've been planning to do this in late summer or early fall. But I think the time is right."

"In the next 45 days?" one of his assistants exclaimed. "That's a short timeframe and is way off track with our planned schedule. What brought this on? Were you struck by lighting or something?"

"Well, I wish I could give you a good concrete reason. But I've been thinking about this, and I think that if we wait, the economic and political conditions will work against us. I believe that everything is lined up for us to get this proposal passed by the board and accepted by the community. My intuition was barking at me. And, no, I wasn't struck by lightning—let's just say I was hit by insight."

With those words, Bower and his staff got to work, refining the pending proposal, cleaning up the numbers, and developing a presentation for the April meeting. This plan, presented months earlier than expected, was passed unanimously and subsequently implemented over the next four years.

Serendipity? A roll of the dice? Shooting from the hip? Was there more to it than that? Was the superintendent aware of some forces in the political, social, and educational context that increased the chances of this proposal passing? Or was it just plain luck?

Actually, Bower was adapting to the circumstances he felt, observed, and anticipated. He was demonstrating a key adaptive behavior: using ongoing feedback about the reality of what's happening and what is possible. He drew upon both data and the intangibles to adjust his leadership strategies. He recognized emerging patterns that caused him to change course. The skill to rely on multisensory feedback and adapt accordingly is crucial to adaptive resilience within the complexity fueled by adversity.

Adaptive leaders see patterns before they become obvious to others. They extract meaning from observations, interactions, data, and other sources. They sort information quickly but also make inferences based on partial information. Leaders seldom, if ever, have *all* the information, particularly in crisis or critical situations. Seeing patterns extends their sight beyond what is immediately before them and gives them foresight into what is unfolding and insight into the dynamic of why things are changing. Identifying patterns puts the larger context *in-formation* and becomes a source of knowledge about the dynamics in interaction

Luke Bower, while thinking about the proposal, was engaging over time in a series of interactions with the school board, the community, and other sectors. He was gathering feedback and information about the economy, budgets, relationships, and political dynamics that caused him to alter his plans to the patterns he was seeing and sensing.

While many leaders see themselves as adaptable, the truth of the matter is many of them live in their comfort zones, which they like and want to maintain. They operate within those comfort zones as much as possible. These zones certainly exist at the highest levels of the organization. In fact, leaders high in the hierarchy are sometimes less flexible because they can become isolated or because they have issues of control. Cocoons can be comfortable, but risky, places. Ignorance from living in the comfort of a cocoon destroys the ability to adapt.

Adaptive leaders always seek information actively from everywhere, including places and sources never considered before. They gather trends and research inside and outside their fields of responsibility providing them with a broader and deeper perspective on what's budding in the larger environment. Information must be circulated freely so people can interpret and use it to foresee what's emerging. Without analyzing information, leaders and their team cannot adapt.

Feedback should give leaders a "whack on the side of the head" and jolt them out of their tunnel vision and comfort zones where leaders delude themselves that they have total control over the events. Some leaders have the illusion they have command to make things happen simply through pronouncements and linear cause-and-effect approaches. They confuse control with regulation, and power with domination. In a sense, the mirage of control gets in the way of adaptive resilience because people think disequilibrium is an abnormality, rather than the natural state. In life the unexpected happens and change is constant, though not always immediately recognizable.

As leaders face current issues another batch of issues is getting ready to surface. Leaders who are easily upset by turbulence may be in the wrong job. Change, and the inherent turmoil with it, is reality. They must willingly embrace it even if the situation is alien to past experience and performance.

Adaptive leaders strengthen organizational adaptability by including other members of the team in problem solving. Certainly, the first step in involvement is to communicate clearly the challenges that confront the group. They expand their skills and insights to address the problem and generate creative solutions. Adaptive leaders are open to opinions and insight of others, recognizing that a preeminent leader involves the right people at the right time to identify possible answers. They revel in the creativity of others. Successful leaders foster independence, helping others use their skills and capacity to produce imaginative solutions.

A newly appointed Connecticut superintendent discovered the hazards of leaders who create dependency in team members. Eileen Selke assumed the job from a superintendent who retired after a long, successful career in the district. His style was characterized by issuing "edicts and orders" that the administrators were directed to implement without question. "My leadership style was a stark contrast for them to adjust to and trust," Selke said. She struggled through a period of silence at meetings due to the team members' fear and apprehension about going on record and making mistakes. Eventually through a series of frustrating meetings and retreats she gained their trust and built "a high functioning team where everyone contributed and shared the load."

As a new superintendent, Selke realized she needed help in the form of ongoing feedback from others to succeed. This realization is crucial for all leaders to discover. Adaptive capacity is strengthened by learning from constant feedback—gathering reactions, making sense of the world, learning about oneself, and gaining a sense of efficacy.

Action Strategy: Resilient Leaders adjust Expectations about what is Possible based on what is Learned about the Reality of the Current Situation

Strategies and expectations are symbiotic bedfellows. As circumstances change, expectations for achievement may have to be revised. Old strategies that produced consistent results may no longer do the job. New dynamics raise new questions. What once was possible may no longer look promising. In other words, as we said in Chapter 2, *shift happens,* compelling expectations to shift also.

Today's leaders live in a context of multiple expectations, launched from all directions and perspectives: teachers, administrators, parents, students, legislators, government officials, senior citizens, ethnic groups, colleagues, and a host of others. Plus, leaders have expectations for themselves. In this atmosphere, conflict is predictable, and finding the right path in this forest of aspirations is not easy or simple.

These shifting expectations pack a powerful punch because people assume action to follow expectation. Shifting conditions require different expectations and approaches. In some cases, new expectations may be more ambitious, rather than more modest. They can emanate from external sources—technology, economics, and politics. Others are hatched internally from the organization's pool of talent and relationships.

Leaders sort through the evolving reality and the layers of expectations and use information and intuition because they have a responsibility to find solutions. One way is to protect creative individuals, those "wolves howling in the wilderness," who might have the right response in the right measure to address the state of affairs. The organization needs new ideas—even those that have not been a part of the discussion before and may at first seem radical. These propositions can shed new light and insight on the issue and what can be achieved.

A new principal in Vermont, Julia Maren, faced the challenge of poor test scores. She felt pressure from the central office to produce results, as did the teachers. She decided to try something different. "I just didn't want the staff to teach to the test and put pressure on the kids. Just teach the curriculum and provide personal attention, I told them. I wanted them to help the kids relax during test days," she reflected. "On the test days, I quietly pumped Mozart into the classrooms, and during breaks we gave the kids snacks of raisins, nuts and fruit. I wanted a relaxed, not pressured life-or-death environment."

Instead of focusing on the test, she highlighted the environment so the kids were serious, but not uptight, fearful, and nauseous. The test scores improved, and, in her opinion, it was in part because she took pressure off the teachers and students so they could do their best. It was a bit unusual from the "high stakes" competitive environment many schools have on test days. "I think for people to do their best, they have to be relaxed and not function with false pressure. After all, our job is to help children do their best and show what they learned. This isn't the Super Bowl."

New strategies and expectations require resourcefulness, pruning stale and impotent processes out of the system—an act of creative destruction. Adaptive leaders prune what does not work so they can find the resources for ideas that do. They build bridges to new concepts, protect individuals with creative ideas, and engage in defining what does not make sense anymore. They adapt and mature, which may result in altered expectations—smaller or greater—than initially anticipated. In summary, resilient leaders move beyond just surviving to thriving in the thick of adversity if they see the world with "new eyes"—as it is—and then find solutions that move outside the rigidity of past practice and obsolete expectations.

Action Strategy: Resilient Leaders Demonstrate the Ability to put Mistakes in Perspective and move Beyond them

We all know what Post-it® Notes are: those little self-stick notepapers. Most people use them and love them. But Post-it® Notes were the product of a failure. They didn't come from a well-oiled intention to devise weak adhesive notepaper. Far from it!

In 1970 Spencer Silver was working in the 3M research laboratories to find a strong adhesive. Silver developed a new adhesive, but it was the reverse of the goal—even weaker than what 3M already manufactured. It stuck to objects, could easily be lifted off, and was super weak instead of super strong. No one knew what to do with the stuff, but Silver didn't discard it.

One Sunday four years later, another 3M scientist, Arthur Fry, who sang in the church's choir, used markers to keep his place in the hymnal. But they kept falling out of the book. Frey remembered Silver's adhesive, and used some to coat his markers. With the weak adhesive, the markers stayed in place, yet lifted off without damaging the pages. Suddenly, out of failure sprung success. 3M began distributing Post-it ® Notes nationwide in 1980, ten years after Silver developed a super weak adhesive, accidentally. Today this failure-turned-success is one of the most popular office products available.

In the world of educational leadership, individuals at all levels are immobilized by the fear of failure. For example, when a class of doctoral students recently was asked about the prospect of assuming a leadership position, the conversation quickly uncovered their fear of failure, not being up to the task. This fear was ingrained in their attachment to being perceived as "competent" and "knowledgeable." "I worry about making mistakes," a young teacher said when thinking about leading a faculty as principal. When probed further, she and others in the class were reticent about taking on a new role, not understanding that failure, at one time or other, follows all leaders.

Making mistakes in judgment and action are a part of the risks leaders take. Changing environments are hazardous in the sense that leaders must walk a new path that takes them through obvious and unknown obstacles or pitfalls. Old strategies may not work, former concepts may not apply, and established structures may actually hamper achieving success.

In these circumstances failure is an option: success is never guaranteed. However, leaders pay a heavy price for failure if it constricts confidence and paralyzes their ability to act. Fear of failure can freeze people into not making decisions. Ego-driven leaders, particularly, may not be willing to jeopardize their reputation or status by pursuing a new course.

So the question is: what should leaders do when confronted by mistakes and failure? Or to paraphrase a phrase popularized in *Who Moved My Cheese?*, "If you could move beyond your fear, what would you do?"

In actuality, leaders' fear of mistakes is overblown. All mistakes are not of equal proportion nor are they as fatal as often imagined. It's not that leaders want or intend to fail intentionally, but there are kernels of learning within each breakdown. Resilient leaders can turn glitches into opportunities and gain wisdom and insight. Unexpected collapses or pursuing imaginative strategies can provide information that creates the ability necessary to succeed in the future.

A learning organization does not fear missteps because there is a willingness to share responsibility and nurture the curiosity to learn how to respond better in the future. People are not punished when strategies or processes fail. Understanding the source of errors is a gift to any leader or organization that wants to adapt to the complexity of the context.

Selke, the Connecticut superintendent, realized that her team, after years of being directed and controlled, was fearful of failure and uncertainty. They were concerned about the effectiveness of and security under a new leadership style. "There wasn't much I could do except focus on the work at hand and use that focus to try to dispel their fears of mistakes and bring the administrators back together as a team."

Her team's fear of errors and failure could lead to unnecessary anxiety and possibly "scapegoating" for the circumstances and outcomes. Feeling guilty about breakdowns and pointing the finger of blame is antithetical to adaptive behavior. Leaders who insist on compliance and control rarely succeed in creating organizations that flexibly adjust to the times. When fear of error is intense, creativity ceases, resulting in more errors, usually by omission and inaction.

As hard as it seems to understand, adaptive leaders find "power in glorious failure" (Pascale, Milleman, & Gioja, pp. 254–255) because failures and innovation go hand-in-hand. A culture of innovation requires it. Leaders who accept failure as part of the process become stronger. For example, breakdowns force leaders to notice things in the environment that can generate advances in the future. This insight encourages the examination of old norms and procedures, spawning innovation and imagination. In very unstable contexts, leaders continually work to find answers because solutions may be temporary or may not work consistently.

Building capacity to continually find what works is essential to stamina and survival. Experimenting with new ideas and strategies provides the opportunity for growth. Instituting pilot programs to test expectations and strategies produces information if the pilot is assessed and new learning is shared. Static processes in a complex environment will not only result in failure, they can lead to the demise of the organization.

Mistakes, however, are painful, especially if they are self-inflicted. Resilient leaders turn that pain into resolve to move ahead tenaciously, building self-confidence along the way. They use the hurt to become better leaders and do not beat themselves up for errors. After all, mistakes will always occur in complex environments. The issue is determining the nature and causes of the breakdown.

Heifetz (1994) identified the importance of reflection for leaders. In tough times, reflecting about the problems and our responses to them is essential. It helps leaders find meaning and insight into reversals and understand the reactions and feelings, decision-making processes, and relationships involved.

In suffering losses, leaders must have the confidence to live well despite those defeats. They must separate themselves from their role and not take failure personally or as an indictment of their worth. Living in the past or becoming glued to losses is detrimental to personal well-being, a resilience strength we discussed in Chapter 6. What a leader does with the experience is what matters, not the fact that the event happened. Finding balance and adapting offers a sense of peace about their efforts.

From reflective practice comes wisdom, and adaptive leaders need it. "The extraction of wisdom from the crucible experience is what distinguishes our successful leaders from those who are broken or burnt out by comparable experiences. In every instance, our leaders carried the gold of meaning away from their crucibles. And they emerged with new tools as well. . . . (T)esting, however dire, is the hard but fertile soil that leads to continued growth, the process that liberates us from the past" (Bennis and Thomas, 2002, 94). Resilient leaders not only learn about the greater context but, very importantly, they learn about themselves.

Action Strategy: Resilient Leaders Search for Workable Strategies to Achieve Positive Results in Difficult Situations

Results and stability are not achieved by imposing control over others and restricting their freedom to think and innovate. It condemns the organization to stale strategies that block adaptive thinking. Resilient leaders challenge conventional thinking. They ask hard questions with the intent to help people rethink their assumptions and stimulate conversation about finding workable solutions to the adversity they face. Asking tough questions gives the issues back to the people, rather than creating dependency on the perspective of the leader alone. People have to respond and become involved.

Questions help people confront the issues and eliminate the penchant to avoid tough situations. Critical questions help distinguish reality from fantasy and place harsh events into perspective. Distinguishing fact from fiction is an act of integrity because it requires people to face the hard truth. Only then can the group begin to formulate workable solutions and identify what cannot be changed and define what can be altered.

Engaging in dialogue like this with team members strengthens the sense of leadership and direction in the organization. Engaging others generates a sense of efficacy, providing a foundation to find different or new solutions.

What this boils down to is creating a high performing, inclusive team. The search for effective strategies requires talent and skill. Effectively blending the leader's personal skills with the talent found among team members enhances the ability to deal with problems. Inclusion connects the talent to problems, which is necessary to develop new strategies.

Even though leaders may surrender some freedom of discretion by engaging with others, new and surprising options and alternatives emerge. An organization reveals itself and its resilience capacity in the nature and structure of relationships, patterns of behavior, beliefs, and methods for accomplishing work (Wheatley, 1996, 81).

School administrator Caleb Harlen, completing his second year, recognized that he "learned to have the courage to reach out to my colleagues, as well as team members, to get another perspective into the issues I was facing. David *(a superintendent in another school system)* gave an insight I never would have considered." He added, "I always perceived superintendents as lone wolves. But I learned that's not true."

Remember that leadership is not "going it alone." While accountable for action, leaders know how to grow talent and find solutions to complex problems. In that sense, leaders find some solace and comfort in a team of creative and imaginative people committed to a common purpose.

Action Strategy: Resilient Leaders Quickly Change Course, as Needed, to Adapt to Rapidly Changing Circumstances

Leaders not only see with new eyes, but also find new pathways to success and sustainability. Changing times and the pressure ambiguity brings may require quickly altering direction and plans. It makes no sense to "stay the course" and follow strategies and methods that lead to a quagmire of failure and stagnation.

As the world shifts below their feet, leaders must know when to abruptly deviate from outmoded and fruitless ways. People expect leaders to be in tune with the times. Resilient leaders know when to suddenly walk off the worn trail to find new paths. Uncharted territory can be tense and dense but also rewarding. In contrast, while familiar and comfortable, old pathways can be catastrophic because of unexpected swings of the social, economic, and political milieu.

Situations *per se* may not be controllable, but they are *leadable*. Tides can be turned. In a nutshell, resilient leaders face adversity and challenge with a sense of wonder. If things are certain, problems discreet, and solutions clear, then "engineering" a situation is warranted. But when faced with ambiguity, no clear answers, and conflicting priorities, quickly adaptive leadership is essential. And that has ramifications.

In times when leaders must go against the grain and quickly change course, it creates conflict by disrupting expectations others have about what was supposed to happen. So why would leaders do this? Referring to the intent of the action strategy above, resilient leaders sometimes quickly change, not for the sake of change, but to adapt to rapidly changing circumstances.

SUMMARY

Leading is not for the faint-of-heart. Leaders walk the razor's edge (Heifetz, 1994). Adaptive leaders jump to the next plateau beyond convention and move past habit that imprisons an organization in a cocoon of self-protection from the environment. In these circumstances, leaders make the tough call—to take a chance, to take responsibility, to be selfless, and to begin something new in order to do the right thing. The crucible in which leaders find themselves provides great opportunity with the risk of second-guessing and conflict.

Leaders understand that disequilibrium is the natural state, requiring continuous growth, changes in approach, and the risk of failure. To stand in one place and hope for a return to the stability of the past will only create failure in the future and possibly decimate the organization. If new paths are not taken, events can overwhelm and swamp the organization, its identity, and purpose.

Leaders see things clearly even though reality may be disorienting at first. They do not live in a fantasy of charismatic heroism or certain futures. They understand that the unexpected happens and that the world does not respond with mathematical certainty to interventions. History demonstrates the dynamic of disequilibrium and the change it has wrought.

Wheatley (1999) summed up the role of leadership in changing and tumultuous times:

> The leader's role is not to make sure that people know exactly what to do and when to do it. Instead, leaders need to ensure that there is strong and evolving clarity about who the organization is. When this clear identity is available, it serves every member of the organization. Even in chaotic circumstances, individuals can make congruent decisions. Turbulence will not cause the organization to dissolve into incoherence.
>
> In this category, we need leaders. But we don't need bosses. We need leaders to help us develop the clear identity that likes the dark moments of confusion. We need leaders to support us as we learn how to live by our values. We need leaders who understand and we are best controlled by concepts that invite our participation, not policies and procedures that curtail our contribution. (p. 131)

Leaders are known for their adaptability by how they function in tumult and turmoil. Those who follow adaptive principles can help others accept the discomfort of the unknown and the lost equilibrium they feel when conditions are changing in significant ways. They fear for their efficacy and they look not for a hero but for someone to explain the story that is unfolding, identify the challenges and strengths and threats, and create an environment where people can work together to find solutions for the common good.

CHARTING YOUR RESILIENCE PROFILE
FOR ADAPTABILITY

To chart your Leader Resilience Profile for *Adaptability,* return to your completed LRP Survey in Chapter 1, then follow these steps:

- For each item number listed, circle your *actual* item response on the chart.
- Determine the *conversion* score for the item, located directly beneath the *actual* number you circled.
- Enter your conversion score in the box on the extreme left of the chart.
- Sum the scores in the left column to determine your Resilience Strength Score for *Adaptability.*
- Observe your individualized score on the continuum from Moderately Low to Very High.

Table 8.1. Adaptability Subscale

Strength: Adaptability

Item #	Item Response	Enter your Conversion Score for the Item
3	If your *actual* item response is: 1 2 3 4 5 6 Then your *conversion* score is: 6 5 4 3 2 1 **enter your conversion score in the box →**	
9	If your *actual* item response is: 1 2 3 4 5 6 Then your *conversion* score is: 6 5 4 3 2 1 **enter your conversion score in the box →**	
15	If your *actual* item response is: 1 2 3 4 5 6 Then your *conversion* score is: 6 5 4 3 2 1 **enter your conversion score in the box →**	
21	If your *actual* item response is: 1 2 3 4 5 6 Then your *conversion* score is: 1 2 3 4 5 6 **enter your conversion score in the box →**	
43	If your *actual* item response is: 1 2 3 4 5 6 Then your *conversion* score is: 1 2 3 4 5 6 **enter your conversion score in the box →**	
64	If your *actual* item response is: 1 2 3 4 5 6 Then your *conversion* score is: 6 5 4 3 2 1 **enter your conversion score in the box →**	
	Strength Score: Adaptability →	

Strength Score Continuum for Adaptability

Resilience Level →	Moderately Low	Moderate	Moderately High	Very High
Score Range →	13–18	19–24	25–30	31–36

Chapter 9

Resilient Leaders Show Courage under Fire

> You gain strength, courage, and confidence by every experience in which you really stop to look fear in the face. You're able to say "I lived through this horror. I can take the next thing that comes along" . . . you must do the thing you think you cannot do.
>
> —Eleanor Roosevelt

A New England school administrator stood in front of a doctoral class in educational leadership and responded to a student's question about the pressures of the job. "The life of a leader is a precarious one, as it should be. Leaders don't walk the shores of certainty and comfort. It is not their way," he said. "True leaders face life and make themselves known to the world. They do not sit on the warm, grassy slopes of anonymity and simply observe. They get involved with their hearts, souls, and spirit to make dreams and principles a reality."

In a nutshell, the school leader summed up the essence of leadership. Resilient leaders act on their convictions courageously. The cliché that leaders are risk takers has credence. As the school administrator indicated to the class, resilient leaders make themselves vulnerable when they expose themselves to the world: their values, their principles, their philosophy, their ethics, and their passion. All of this takes courage because it strikes at the core of their being and purpose. And it requires a commitment of involvement and action that is not always easy.

Courage comes from the French word for heart, *coeur*. When people act with courage and persevere, they are said to have "heart." Courage has little to do with analysis or strategic planning. Margaret Wheatley (2005) stated, "As much as we may fear emotions at work, leaders need to be willing to let

133

their hearts open and to tell stories that open other people's hearts" (p. 129). One could say that courageous leadership is an affair of the heart.

Courage and resilience are strongly coupled. In today's world leaders need courage over time because leaders confront continual surprises and challenges. Struggling with adversity, staying on course and fulfilling the values of the organization require will and mettle—quiet courage as well as public fortitude. Continued effort in the face of defeat and the willingness to persevere under severe and sometimes wilting stress has always been at the core of leadership. We now turn to specific strategies that support leaders in this struggle to act on the courage of their convictions.

ACTION STRATEGIES FOR COURAGEOUS LEADERSHIP

Action Strategy: Resilient Leaders take Appropriate Action, even when some Things about the Situation are Ambiguous or Confusing

The world is not a predictable place, except the predictability that ambiguity and chaos will be part of leaders' lives. This condition has been referred to as the "butterfly effect," where small, unanticipated actions create explosive waves of effects and commotion (Wheatley, 2005). The complex economic, social, political, and technological context brings uncertainty and surprises— the challenge of living in "interesting," if not perilous, times.

Taking appropriate action under these conditions requires leaders to overcome their fears and help others do the same. In our interview with David Kleinhorst, the superintendent reinforced the relationship between exposure and courage, "The one constant in this job is that you can't hide," Kleinhorst declared. "It's easy to wear everyone else's monkeys. But, you can't let it get to you. You have to face tough issues wherever you go and deal with them."

Several principles (Wheatley, 2005) guide the work of leaders who strive to act with certainty in uncertain times. Resilient leaders understand that:

- Uncertainty is a part of life—the world is ever changing and good things and bad things come and go. Life is also cyclical moving from the new to the old.
- People are interconnected and in perilous times must turn towards each other and build strong relationships.
- Meaning motivates people: leaders remind us why we are doing our work, what mission we are serving, and what we hope to accomplish.
- Goodness and the human spirit are fundamental to being human. They are hopeful and resilient qualities.

- Frantic and fearful activity only creates more chaos. Reflection is important to learn and to meet our destiny. Finding peace of mind and silence are essential for leaders to live out their values.

As leaders confront tough challenges, they must ask hard questions about themselves. In the words of poet David Whyte (2001), "What are we afraid of, what stops us from speaking out and claiming the life we want for ourselves? Quite often it is a sudden horrific understanding of the intimate and extremely personal nature of the exploration. When we ask in a serious manner for those marvelous outer abstracts of courage, captaincy, and greatness, we set in motion an exploration that tests us to the very core. We suddenly realize the intensely personal nature of all these attributes."

Whyte knows that while leaders call for change, they also must change themselves. They must shed "old baggage" to make room for new baggage they inevitably will collect. Once they step off the curb and accept the responsibility of leading others, they risk their most precious hopes and dreams. That isn't easy because it involves their deeply held passion, values, and beliefs. And with that comes threat and fear in the face of the unknown.

Certainly taking appropriate action in tough circumstances is no task for those easily intimidated. This is not to say that fear is alien to leaders because it certainly is not. Fear is a part of leadership. Challenges and uncertainty can provoke a number of fears, which manifest themselves in many ways. When faced with the unknown, some people withdraw, others focus on security, and many become defensive. All fear falling short when things are toughest. Denying the existence of fear can be destructive to the leader as well as the organization.

Drake Sinclair, a Midwestern superintendent, faced his own fear surrounded by complex, ambiguous circumstances, when he led his district through an e-coli outbreak that spread through the district. As he recounted the crisis: "It happened so fast. We started with 28 children diagnosed and then we had 10 more the next day. We had four kids in the hospital on dialysis, with the possibility that some of them would not survive. This was a tough time that lasted more than a month."

When we asked Sinclair if he was fearful of the outcomes, his reply was simple, "Damned right! I was scared. We would go visit the kids in the hospital and it was awful. This kind of adversity just sucks the life out of you."

Sinclair continued with a description of the ambiguity district leaders faced and what they did about it, "What I didn't anticipate from this was the amount of time and uncertainty in trying to find out if our food service was at fault, or even just exactly what happened. So when you have that ambiguity hanging out there and you are trying to communicate accurately to the community through the press it gets messy."

Sinclair successfully managed the mess and the district came through the crisis in good shape. "It was a great learning experience for me. We had to move ahead without all of the information, and we worked closely with other agencies to make the best decisions possible. But I am sure glad it is over." Sinclair and others in his district stood tall and confronted the e-coli outbreak swiftly.

Walking straight into adversity takes strength because the wall of isolation between leaders and those they lead collapses. Unexpected feelings and "undiscussables"—those elephants in the room people ignore because of discomfort or fear—are uncovered. This type of vulnerability takes boldness and courage to confront. However, dancing around issues, dodging responsibility for actions, and not facing people directly when things are tough generates cynicism and doubt.

Leaders must also confront their own attachments. For example, some leaders who are wed to competence fear taking risks that are essential to success. So they play it safe, embracing past practice, or preserving their image of competence. This may be particularly a concern for inexperienced leaders.

Many leaders suffer from the attachment to approval. Everyone has a desire for love and admiration. But like all virtues, there's a dark side to approval. Leaders can lose themselves in the pursuit of the endorsement of others—board members, staff, colleagues, teachers, and unions. Attempting to meet the diverse expectations of all groups endangers credibility or gives the impression of spinelessness. Leaders cannot meet everyone's expectations because many of them are inherently contradictory, nor can they lead by formally or informally polling opinion and pursuing the most popular option.

Responding in an appropriate, timely, and effective manner is essential. Coalescing people around a common goal is difficult because many organizations are fractured into skinny, high-rise silos of departments, specialties, and interests. Competition within the organization can be as fierce and brisk as competition from outside. In many organizations people work separately together, often competitively and without real contact or communication across silos.

Even with current technology, leaders do not always have information nor do they share it with others. Emails can bury leaders and Blackberries can overheat. Minor issues explode into major ones; and people's patience dwindles in nanoseconds. In addition, the public discourse has become less civil, focusing on personalities not problems or solutions. At times it seems everyone wants to win, even at the expense of principles.

Action Strategy: Resilient Leaders always take Prompt, Principled Action on Unexpected Threats before they Escalate out of Control

Successful leaders anticipate threats and opportunities. They do so by understanding driving forces and dynamics, being alert to what is happening in other fields and research, thinking like a prosecuting attorney by mastering the pros and cons of an issue, and just plain active listening. They can help avert crises by preparing people and setting the organizational stage for options and possibilities. This type of strategic thinking can help leaders make prompt decisions if any of the negative options begins to play out.

The expression that leaders need a vision has become overplayed and underdeveloped because it still leaves hanging the question- what kind of vision? Some leaders are skilled at hindsight and looking through the rear view mirror. Others are nearsighted and can't see the forest for the trees. In contrast there are leaders who are farsighted but can't see what's in front of their nose. Resilient leaders need insight the most, particularly in times of adversity. This skill is a prerequisite for having the foresight to prepare for the unexpected.

Foresight, having an idea of what is about to emerge, not simply what is already obvious, is a mark of a resilient leader. It is the capacity to understand what matters and what is temporary by using cognitive analytic and synthesis abilities, as well as intuition, to discern reality and its path. As we have established in earlier chapters, unexpected forces and events certainly upset the status quo. But they should not ripple through the organization doing damage and creating greater adversity. While unexpected consequences cannot be specifically defined, the process for addressing them should be in place.

"We didn't anticipate the economy dropping through the floor," Phil Streeter, a school superintendent in an urban district in New Jersey said. "But we had worked through a number of scenarios reflecting increasing shortfalls. As we worked through them we were able to respond to the town board quickly to their questions and proposed cuts. We presented to them our rationale based upon what we believe is essential to meet our mission and purpose." The foresight Streeter demonstrated through scenario planning prepared the leadership team to make timely recommendations for cuts anchored to core values inherent in the program.

In summary, effective school leaders do not plan their moves day-to-day in any arena, fiscally, programmatically, or procedurally. If they did they would not be able to stave off the bumps in the road or avoid road washouts.

In a sense resilient leaders are like chess masters in a stressful environment. They anticipate a number of moves ahead before they are made and prepare strategies to meet them before things escalate out of control.

Action Strategy: Resilient Leaders make Principled Decisions that, at times, are Contrary to Respected Advice by Others

Leaders with character act with honor beyond their own self-interests for the benefit of the common good. Winston Churchill said, "Courage is rightly esteemed the first of human qualities . . . because it is the quality which guarantees all others." Courage is the foundation that underlies all of the virtues. Without courage, other values cannot live. But courage isn't easy. Trauma and losses cause some leaders to lose the courage to stand up with integrity.

Courage and character are frequently referred to as "having backbone," which requires resilience coupled with strength of purpose—both essential to the concept of character. In the heat of controversy and struggle, courageous leaders remain steady in their principles and don't fall prey to the forces that want to deter them from doing what is right. They are driven by principle, not their own attachment to popularity, position, standing or security. Nor do they succumb to the advice of colleagues or others if it is contrary to their values and principles.

A veteran superintendent faced controversy when the district test scores failed to meet state standards. He was justifiably worried about school board and community reaction because the district had been making progress and the investment in new programs was considerable in money and time.

An assistant superintendent offered a way to moderate the community's reaction. "Let's use several charts—graphs. They will be accurate, but we can manipulate the left axis on the data charts so the decline doesn't look so large. The public will pay more attention to the charts than a bunch of written explanations."

The superintendent looked at him with fire in his eyes. "I'm not into manipulating data that distorts the true picture. We are going to give them the whole story about the test results—straight. No doubletalk." He could have fudged the chart, but didn't. He was clear about his core values and he drew upon them in deciding the ethical approach to handling the adversity. The leader demonstrated confidence and competence that doing the right thing would successfully lead the district through any disagreement.

This superintendent acted with virtue and in accord with his true nature. He used his judgment and weighed the circumstances through the lens of principle. Great leaders affirm their principles in crisis and conflicting times. Those who succumb to fear, ego, or insecurity end up with compromised principles and are seen as event-driven manipulators. In short, they lose credibility. Standing on principles and rising above the politics of others' self-interest is truly a self-affirming act of courage.

As we illustrated in Chapter 3 with the Personal Strengths Triangle, character, credibility, and authenticity are cemented together. "Leading with character gives the wise leader clear-cut advantages. They are easier to trust and follow; they honor commitments and promises; their words and character match; they are always engaged in and by the world; they are open to 'reflective backtalk'; they admit errors and learn from their mistakes. They can speak with conviction because they believe in what they're saying. They are comfortable in their own skin. They feel at ease in the spotlight and enjoy it there. They tend to be more open to opportunity and risk" (Tichy and Bennis, 2007, p. 84). The virtues culminate in the strength to take action that runs counter to the advice by others.

Action Strategy: Resilient Leaders always take Prompt, Decisive Action in Emergency Situations Demanding an Immediate Response

Courageous leaders and crisis are almost synonymous. In tough situations, they adopt the style of leadership required, inform themselves as best they can, act with *prudent* dispatch, and then stand tall in the face of inevitable scrutiny that follows.

A Midwestern superintendent, Claire Addison, talked, with much emotion, about a crisis she faced, the murder of a principal in school while class was in session. The superintendent described the horrid details.

"The perpetrator was unknown and the school was in 'lock-down' for over two hours. I was in a conference with an elementary principal when I got the call that a principal at the high school had been shot! I sat back in the chair in total disbelief—a whole series of images flashed before my eyes. In an instant, I reacted and gave some instructions to Scott, who made the call to me, to stay at the central office, leave a phone line open, gather the central staff, and contact the 15 other schools in the district to kick in the crisis plan. I told him I would call him later on the open line so we could communicate. I then headed to the school. I couldn't believe what was happening, but I remember being calm and focused."

When the superintendent arrived, the police and emergency personnel were there, information was unfolding slowly, and the staff locked in the office were in emotional shock. "Occasionally, brief shimmers of feeling broke through the cocoon I placed around my emotions when all hell was breaking loose. But honestly, I don't know how I got through those first few hours," he recollected. "I felt removed like I was having an out of body experience watching things unfold and just reacting."

In these cases decisiveness in decisions is critical, using wisdom and judgment in both the content and execution of crisis plans. Every crisis decision includes substance, a central core that is the content of a decision—the "whats" of the decision. Substance concerns the impact of the result on the mission, desired outcomes, or direction of the organization. Substantive judgments usually are about content of programs, management, and accountability.

Tactical decisions answer a different question: "How are we going to implement the substance of the decision?" Tactics and strategy are the main emphases in putting a substantive decision into action.

In emergency situations wise judgment is essential on both substantive and tactical levels. A wise substantive decision can fail because of tactics and timing. Conversely, a poor decision can be implemented in a timely and very effective manner with mediocre or disastrous results. Successful decisions require insightful and mature judgment on substance, tactics, and timeliness.

Almost all substantive or tactical decisions in the midst of crisis will evoke controversy. Decisions frequently are challenged or second-guessed, usually after the immediate heat of the crisis has dissipated. Crises come in various forms, such as weather emergencies, budget crises, discipline incidents, threats, and even violent acts. But one thing is constant. Crisis will happen. Resilient leaders must respond appropriately under severe pressure by defining the problem, finding viable options, selecting an appropriate substantive solution, and implementing an effective tactical approach—all in a timely manner.

Crises require calmness and assuredness. There is no room for self-doubts or status concerns. Wise leaders know that people will challenge their actions. They also know that in a crisis there are no easy answers or the luxury of time to mull over options before they define a direction. Decisions must be made efficiently, often without all of the information at hand. Leaders have to make a prompt decision with the information they have—even if it is sketchy, contrary, and difficult to verify.

The inevitable complexity of leading in emergency conditions does not deter others from exercising their self-declared "right" to second-guess the leaders. Often, the "Monday morning quarterbacks" challenge the timing of decisions and the subsequent execution. The correct decision, implemented too late can lead to disaster, just as much as a wrong decision pursued promptly can be catastrophic. No wonder that many leaders claim they need extra compensation for hazardous duty pay. Claims aside, resilient leaders prepare to anticipate the unanticipated and have crisis plans in place, ready to be activated if the need arises.

Action Strategy: Resilient Leaders Seek Perspectives that Differ Significantly from their own, so they can make the most Informed Decisions Possible under Tough Conditions

Defining moments can come in a whirl or they can gestate awhile, waiting for a reaction. In either case, courageous leaders must seek and understand different perspectives.

Sometimes in adversity people fragment, hiding behind roles, creating boundaries, or imposing regulations and controls. Isolation and withdrawal happen when people disengage with each other. They construct walls rather than bridges, and jeopardize relationships and limit input.

As stated before, isolation is an impediment to good judgment. Isolated leaders shortchange their insight and perspective. They become prisoners of past successful strategies or fall victim to the arrogance of ego.

Some leaders find it hard to ask for help, feeling that there is an expectation that they are infallible. The superintendent in the small Connecticut town, Eileen Selke, summarized it well. "Leaders are expected to be infallible . . . we are expected to practice a 'don't let them see you sweat' philosophy. But in truth, we are only human. I have to remember sometimes that to be resilient, you just have to ask for help. You have to be willing to seek out the support of others in whatever shape that may take. You don't have to carry the weight of the world on your shoulders all by yourself. In fact, to do so is self-destructive."

The art of conversation, one of the oldest methods of all time, is an invaluable tool for leaders to get input and insight into different positions and perceptions—to share different ideas and divergent viewpoints. Listening actively to others' perspectives, both the content and intent of the messages, builds understanding and connections that may be constructive in the present and sets the stage for future conversations.

Through conversation, leaders build webs of networks through which ideas are shared, examined, and challenged. These networks can be open highways for probing issues, as well as an essential means for scrutinizing ideas to discover fresh approaches.

Conversation requires courageous speech—speaking from the heart, addressing aspirations and hopes, results and values, principles and practice, and dreams and reality. What greater act of respect can leaders show than to listen to their coworkers and colleagues? How else can they tap the dormant creativity, talent, and imagination of the people working with them? Aren't resilient leaders stronger by encouraging diverse perspectives rather than suppressing them?

Relationships and conversations are not immune to inappropriate, offensive, and obnoxious behavior. People can give the wrong advice or make mistakes. When this happens, what is the leader's role? How do leaders bring wholeness back to relationships that are difficult or strained? The options are to let them deteriorate further to the detriment of the organization or to try to heal them.

To be resilient, leaders have to forgive—themselves, others, and circumstances. As one school leader from Illinois told us, "I think practicing forgiveness is an important skill. It is a life lesson, but it also comes in handy in trying to be sure that you can go on the next day." As an illustration, this leader described a time when he was "horrified" by the conduct of the teachers when they removed all of the children's work from bulletin boards as a collective job action to protest budget cuts. But he ultimately engaged in forgiveness, not retribution. He explained why, "In order for the teachers to respect me I have to convey respect for them. So being upset and angry and disbelieving is something that I had to work through and get over. The only way to do that was through forgiveness."

As the Illinois school leader demonstrated, risking forgiveness is an act of strength, not a benign or softheaded one. Anyone can saber rattle, threaten, and berate to intimidate. But authentically courageous leaders forgive so they can move ahead and not live in the past surrounded by former hurts, antagonisms, or revenge.

SUMMARY

Having a vision of the future requires constructing bridges, and not having past events dictate the future. Existing behind the walls of what went before, creating illusions, and living with the paranoia of mistakes is self-destructive conduct. Leadership is living in the moment, looking to the future, and not getting mired in what went before. Resilient leaders act on principle and values with moral courage, make timely, appropriate decisions in crisis, and consider the contributions of others by being humble enough to realize that help is available.

One of the most prominent and acclaimed writers on leadership, James MacGregor Burns (1978) wrote about principled leadership: "leaders and followers are locked into relationships that are closely influenced by particular, local, parochial, regional, and cultural forces. In the progression of both leaders and followers through stages of needs, values, and morality, leaders find a broadening and deepening base from which they can reach out to widening social collectives to establish and embrace 'higher' values and principles" (p. 429). Without principles, you do not have courage.

Courage is needed in today's climate to do the right thing, to step out, to go against the grain of convention if necessary. Leaders innovate and take hold in crisis and tragedy. They have a high standard to reach in these circumstances. Their credibility and integrity are on the line. They must act appropriately and promptly, engage others in finding solutions, provide strong guidance and support, and use all of their knowledge and procedural and interpersonal skill. People count on them to do the right thing.

CHARTING YOUR RESILIENCE PROFILE FOR COURAGEOUS DECISION-MAKING

To chart your Leader Resilience Profile for *Courageous Decision-Making,* return to your completed LRP Survey in Chapter 1, then follow these steps:

- For each item number listed, circle your *actual* item response on the chart.
- Determine the *conversion* score for the item, located directly beneath the *actual* number you circled.
- Enter your conversion score in the box on the extreme right column of the chart.
- Sum the scores in the right column to determine your Resilience Strength Score for *Courageous Decision-Making.*
- Observe your individualized score on the continuum from Moderately Low to Very High.

Table 9.1. Courageous Decision-Making Subscale

Strength: Courageous Decision-Making

Item #	Item Response	Enter your Conversion Score for the Item
5	If your *actual* item response is: 1 2 3 4 5 6 Then your *conversion* score is: 6 5 4 3 2 1 **enter your conversion score in the box →**	
11	If your *actual* item response is: 1 2 3 4 5 6 Then your *conversion* score is: 6 5 4 3 2 1 **enter your conversion score in the box →**	
17	If your *actual* item response is: 1 2 3 4 5 6 Then your *conversion* score is: 6 5 4 3 2 1 **enter your conversion score in the box →**	
23	If your *actual* item response is: 1 2 3 4 5 6 Then your *conversion* score is: 1 2 3 4 5 6 **enter your conversion score in the box →**	
24	If your *actual* item response is: 1 2 3 4 5 6 Then your *conversion* score is: 6 5 4 3 2 1 **enter your conversion score in the box →**	
42	If your *actual* item response is: 1 2 3 4 5 6 Then your *conversion* score is: 6 5 4 3 2 1 **enter your conversion score in the box →**	
	Strength Score: Courageous Decision-Making →	

Strength Score Continuum for Courageous Decision-Making

Resilience Level →	Moderately Low	Moderate	Moderately High	Very High
Score Range →	13–18	19–24	25–30	31–36

Chapter 10

Resilient Leaders Pledge: Hold Me Responsible

Action springs not from thought, but from a readiness for responsibility.

—Dietrich Bonhoeffer

It is not only for what we do that we are held responsible, but also for what we do not do.

—John Baptiste Moliére

Leaders live on the point. When they assume a position of authority, they are expected to accept professional and personal responsibility for their own conduct, decisions, and mistakes along the road to achievement. Being on the point also means that leaders are ultimately accountable for the short- and long-term care of the organization they lead.

The burden of responsibility for today's leaders is extremely heavy. Many would argue that the load limit on the shoulders of leaders increased exponentially when "standards-based" metrics became a critical measure of leadership performance. With such weighty issues on the table, leaders feel the personal weight of being expected to know enough, become skillful enough, and to remain healthy enough to get the job done right, done with integrity, and done with the type of leadership that will strengthen organizational resilience.

The purpose of this chapter is to offer some help to leaders as they struggle to stay upright under the enormous weight of their responsibilities. First we examine the many faces of *personal responsibility*. Then we outline specific strategies that leaders can implement to help them be more resilient and lead with honor in times of turmoil.

THE MULTIPLE FACES OF RESPONSIBILITY

The term *personal responsibility* consists of multi-faceted dimensions. First, leaders are personally responsible to themselves to conduct their lives in line with their deepest moral principles. They also have a moral obligation to take responsibility for district outcomes in the area of academic performance. Finally, by virtue of their job description, leaders bear a heavy responsibility for the long-term vitality of the organization.

Most job announcements don't spell out these responsibilities in detail, if at all. But the leadership expectations in these areas are real and demanding. When challenged or severely criticized, resilient leaders take the high road by taking responsibility and avoiding the easier path leading to victim status. In this section we address each of the facets listed and indicate the interrelationship among them.

Moral Responsibility

When leaders first dive into the murky water of high expectations, immediately they are pulled in all directions by the currents of politics, economics, and self-interests. But each morning they have to look at themselves in the mirror. If they have succumbed to assorted forces that try to drag them away from their personal core values, they will not like what they see.

As an antidote to these pressures, resilient leaders work hard to stay attuned to their moral compass pointing toward responsible leadership. Personal responsibility begins within. Leaders who discover their calling—their reason for leading—find fulfillment in their role. They know themselves in the deepest way—their beliefs, philosophy, and needs. It is the difficult, but necessary, work of all leaders. Know thyself includes the ability to clarify one's own highest priority values and to articulate these values to others. In Chapter 3 we discussed strategies for making this happen.

Personal responsibility is not synonymous with taking everything personally. Sometimes it is difficult for leaders to differentiate between themselves as individuals and their professional role as leaders. If they take criticism and events personally, they can be blown off course by the emotions of the moment. Criticism, like adversity, is inevitable. It comes with the territory. How leaders respond is optional. Heifetz (1994) offered several practical suggestions for how to respond to maintain moral integrity:

• Distinguish your *self* from your role as leader.
• Externalize, not internalize, conflict.
• Use partners and colleagues to provide support and feedback.

- Listen to yourself—your feelings, your body, your intuition.
- Find a sanctuary and reflect and think.
- Get on the balcony and see the big picture—don't perseverate on unimportant matters.
- Preserve your sense of purpose.

Leaders who heed Heifetz' advice will discover they are on the road to leading with moral responsibility.

Personal Accountability for Results

Resilient leaders not only know themselves they also know the high stakes involved in leading an organization to perform consistent with expectations held by the community and the standards established at the state and national level. The proverbial bottom line is that leaders have an organizational accountability, a sense of duty, to deliver on results.

Accountability has two components. Reaching measurable targets is obvious. Metrically quantifiable outcomes such as test scores, attendance and discipline records, fiscal statistics, and other data have been emphasized in standards and legislative mandates.

But leaders are also responsible for more than the *what*. They are responsible for the *how,* how to get the job done using strategies that have met the litmus test of proven best-practices. Methods and approaches are intertwined with the first facet we discussed, moral purpose. Metrics achieved without a strong philosophical base can breach ethical and moral standards. The ends do not validate the means: results garnered through fear and coercion become hollow, short-lived, and damaging to the resilience of the organization as well as the leaders.

Max Weber expressed accountability for leaders very well. "It is immensely moving when the mature man—no matter whether old or young in years—is aware of the responsibility for the consequences of his conduct and really feels such responsibility with heart and soul . . . somewhere he reaches the point where he says 'Here I stand; I can do no other.'" Reaching this point takes strength of character and purpose to stand tall on accepting responsibility for organizational results.

Service Responsibility

Moral responsibility and organizational accountability are intertwined with the third dimension of leadership responsibility, stewardship of service. As Goens (2005) described in his book entitled, *Soft Leadership for Hard Times,* during difficult times both the organization and the community need the soft side that leaders manifest through their compassion, caring, and support. Resilient leaders are passionate about their duty of service to colleagues, the profession, the organization, and self. They feel a strong obligation to the common good and not just what is good for powerful selfish interests fighting to protect their own turf. This orientation has an altruistic dimension to it. Leaders, as stewards, help others even when there is nothing to be gained for them personally.

In fulfilling their duty, leaders are fundamentally responsible for the strength and success of people in the organization. They exercise power and mobilize the energy of others to address problems in a principled way through clear and appropriate values. They help others develop a greater strength of purpose that aligns with organizational purpose and mission.

Bringing purpose to life is a leader's responsibility, personally, organizationally, and communally. The interplay of these three dimensions converges into leadership actions shaped by the answers to these questions:

- Are our actions and values congruent?
- What enduring legacy will we leave behind for the organization?
- Is the decision just and fair?
- Does the system maintain credibility?
- Have we maximized our resources to meet our purpose?
- Is the organization's well-being and sustainability enhanced?

To respond to these questions in a responsible way, resilient leaders align their beliefs with specific actions such as the ones discussed below.

ACTION STRATEGIES TO STRENGTHEN
PERSONAL RESPONSIBILITY

Action Strategy: Resilient Leaders Accept Responsibility for making Tough Choices that may Negatively Affect some Individuals or Groups

Organizational adversity typically involves complex issues with multiple possible options as resolution. Leading has never been claimed to be easy. In today's turbulent times, veteran leaders say it is even getting harder. As one school principal lamented, "My teacher friends tell me, 'quit whining about tough decisions. That's why you get paid the big bucks.' I guess, in this case, perception is reality. And I can't argue with another point my friend made when he said making the tough calls is why leaders are called leaders. It's hard to argue with his view. That's just life in the fast lane of leadership."

Fainthearted or indecisive leaders can drive themselves to distraction and even shirk their responsibility to act. Strong leaders want to face those daunting decisions because those judgments are the ones that produce the momentum to confront the turmoil and move ahead.

Tough choices are decisive events. They come packaged in a number of different wrappings and distinctive bows. All of them, however, require choices around ideals and principles and become judgments anchored by ethical integrity. Ethical dilemmas between right and wrong aren't usually agonizing ones. Leaders do what is right. Ethical judgments become tougher when they involve the collision of two or more positive values requiring strong principles compass and character. Take, for example, the ethical collisions inherent in dire economic circumstances that pit rising costs of special education with the escalating costs of "regular" education. Should administrators spend substantial sums of money on the education of a smaller segment of the student population at the expense of providing programming for the large majority of students? In difficult times, what choices are available and which ones will leaders make?

In the ideal world, school leaders would like to do both—but that may not be possible. "My special education budget is out of control," a Midwest school leader exclaimed. "I spend about twenty-three percent of the budget on ten percent of the kids. Should I cut regular education programs for all kids to meet the needs of one small segment of our students? It's tough. The budget will not pass as is. The rising cost of special education outplacements is killing us."

This leader faces a highly volatile leadership dilemma, reflecting a predicament encountered by his colleagues across the nation. Parents of both special and regular education students want the best for their children and will demand free and appropriate education to meet their children's individual needs. In addition revenues may be decreasing and taxes increasing along with a stifling economy and high unemployment.

Another tough decision leaders face entails serving the common good at the expense of the self-interest of a few. Failure to adequately satisfy the needs of a powerful, highly influential constituency in order to serve the common good of the community likely will cost the leader political capital and possibly job security. For leaders, courageous decisions are not impact neutral. They can exact a toll personally and professionally.

These moments have three characteristics, according to Badaracco (1997): "They reveal, they test, and they shape. In other words, a right versus right decision can reveal a manager's basic values, and, in some cases, those of an organization. At the same time, the decision tests the strength of the commitments that a person or an organization has made. Finally, the decision casts a shadow forward. It shapes the character of the person and, in some cases, the organization" (p. 7).

A former Massachusetts superintendent, Gary Millard, had to make severe budget cuts. He faced the unfortunate task of deciding which productive program would have to be scratched. He said, "It really cut my heart out. Over three years I had to slash over a million dollars out of a relatively small district budget. We started to go in reverse—we even got to the point of cutting all-day kindergarten. That was tough . . . none of those decisions were easy. All the things we cut had value."

In these circumstances, supporters will say, "The leader stood up for the correct principles." The critics predictably will declare, "See that ridiculous decision proved once again that the so-called leader buckles under the pressure of the squeaky wheel." Right versus right issues can polarize people advocating on both sides of the argument. There is no middle ground in a principle to please everyone with a "half a loaf"—a choice must be made.

These "defining" decisions, according to Badaracco, "typically involve choices between two or more courses of action, each of which is a complicated bundle of ethical responsibilities, personal commitments, moral hazards, and practical pressures and constraints" (p. 6). These decisions are strong markers of a leader's integrity to principles and values and undeniable tests of the credibility with different constituencies.

Action Strategy: Resilient Leaders Realize that not taking Action in the Face of Adversity Carries with it Personal Responsibility for that Action

This strategy can also be stated as, "No decision is, in fact, a decision, and the leader is equally accountable for these nondecisions."

In some cases, a decision by a leader not to act turns out to be an act of avoidance. Marty Schein, a middle school principal in a suburban Southwest district, was told by the Assistant Superintendent for Human Resources to notify all first-year teachers in the school that they likely would be reassigned next year. The district was tentatively planning to open a new middle school and teachers would have to be reassigned to align with the reassignment of students at the middle school level. The principal had hired these teachers and considered them to be among the most talented on the staff. Schein also heard that the new school may not be ready in time for next year, so he chose to take a wait-and-see attitude.

In July, during a period when the principals were off contract, the school board announced at a board meeting the school would open as planned, and they released the names of teachers who would be reassigned. Not surprisingly the affected teachers at Schein's school were irate at the lack of notice. They confronted the school board about the surprise, who in turn confronted the superintendent, and the chain reaction of blame finally landed on Schein's desk.

Schein offered this in defense of his inaction, "I was just trying to protect the teachers from unwarranted agony in case the new school didn't open on time." He pleaded that he didn't take the wrong action. He just delayed making the right decision. That rationalization didn't work. He was held accountable for not following the administrative directive. His decision not to decide was a leadership action that adversely affected others, and was reflected in his annual performance review.

In other contexts, deciding by inaction is appropriate. A suburban Midwest superintendent received a phone call from a principal. He had just met with parents who accused a male teacher of inappropriate contact with their daughter. As the superintendent described the situation, "Steve called on Thursday with the problem and said while the parents were 'not off the wall' they were absolutely adamant that something be done soon. Steve concurred and diffused the parents' anger temporarily by removing the teacher from the classroom. I told him that we shouldn't take any action immediately. We had to consider the facts, determine what is morally and legally right, and then decide. I told him, 'By next week we should have enough information and things will be clearer about what to do.' Knee jerking, particularly in this case, was not the right course. Safety wasn't an issue because the teacher was removed from the classroom until a thorough investigation could be conducted. Too much was at stake, I thought, and we had to be patient in deciding. Too often when we get complaints, we think being responsive is doing something fast. Sometimes taking action translates into the action of thinking about it for a while."

In both cases described above, the leaders had a choice: take action or decide not to act. In all cases, leaders are charged with making deliberate decisions, including the option to do nothing. And they will be held accountable for the outcomes of the decision, not just for the intentions or specific action chosen. In tough times, resilient leaders reach decisions, including the decision not to act, that align with their moral responsibility, their accountability obligations, and their commitment to stewardship of service.

Action Strategy: Resilient Leaders accept Accountability for the long-term Organizational Impact of any Tough Leadership Decision they Make

Some difficult decisions pivot on the fulcrum between short-term results and long-term stewardship. Thinking long-term, especially in crisis conditions, poses serious short-term hazards for leaders. In the midst of turmoil, people may push for quick-fix answers to hopefully alleviate some of the existing pain and chaos. Admittedly it isn't easy to reject the appearance of immediate decisiveness for long-term wisdom: to pass up ready praise for deferred respect. However, popular, short-term actions can jeopardize making choices that serve the long-term sustainability of the organization. One is a true act of stewardship and the other is a concession to immediate popularity.

Stewardship translates into creating an organization that will sustain itself over time and realize its mission. Resilient leaders who accept the account-ability of stewardship also accept the principles of maintaining due diligence, meeting obligations honestly, and maintaining integrity with the institution's overarching purpose. This includes accepting responsibility for decisions made by a leader's supervisor, including the school board, as well as those individuals the leader supervises.

Consider, for example, a situation where the school board directed the administration to redraw attendance boundaries at the high school level because of the pending opening of a third high school. The superintendent appointed the assistant superintendent for human resources as chair of the committee, charged with making recommendations to the superintendent and, ultimately, the board.

After several months of deliberation, the committee reached consensus on a set of boundary changes, consistent with the guidelines drawn up by the district and approved by the school board. In presenting committee recom-mendations to the superintendent, the assistant superintendent expressed con-fidence that the plan was the right thing to do. The superintendent reflected and then responded, "It is the right thing to do. But it will be voted down by the board for political reasons. It redistributes a neighborhood filled with powerful movers and shakers in the community, sending the students to three different high schools. I think we need to find another 'right' plan that will fly politically. Otherwise all of the committee work will be flushed down the toilet."

The assistant superintendent wouldn't budge on the recommendations. They had fulfilled their charge, in his professional judgment, and what happened after that wasn't the committee's problem. This position caused several problems for the superintendent. He felt morally responsible to take actions that will have a positive, long-term impact on the organization and the community. He also felt a responsibility to support his administrative team if they act in accord with their charge. And, finally, but no less important, he accepted a moral obligation to implement with integrity any decision that the board made. So he reluctantly agreed to submit the boundary plan, intact, to the board.

Predictably, the board listened to all of the angry, powerful voices in the community. Their actions generated hostility across neighborhoods as harsh, unfair statements circulated about the "haves" and the "have-nots" stereotypes of certain neighborhood communities.

The conclusion was not what the superintendent hoped for but what he predicted. After supporting the committee's recommendations, the superintendent endured the wrath of the board for putting them in an untenable position, and the blame escalated throughout the community, directed primarily at the superintendent. The board devised their own boundary plan, one that satisfied the powerhouse constituencies. Finally the superintendent's credibility was weakened in the eyes of the board and the community elite. All of this made it more difficult for the superintendent to make tough decisions in the future that would carry with it a positive, long-term impact on the organization.

Resilient leaders, above all else, need to be true to their ethical convictions. At the highest level of ethical principles, the superintendent should not compromise his actions if there was *only* one right plan. But if it is a matter of choosing among several plans that would work without violating ethical principles, leaders may have to compromise one value, such as supporting administrative staff, to honor a higher order value such maintaining his credibility to lead the organization into the future.

Action Strategy: Resilient Leaders Acknowledge Mistakes in Judgment and Assume Responsibility for making the Necessary changes in the Future

Virtually all effective leaders have established a track record of success on a life-long foundation of "being right." They did the right things as children. They had the right answers in school. They moved into entry-level leadership assignments early in their career because, within their peer group, they seemed to have the so-called "rightest" perspective much of the time.

By the time leaders reach more visible, high profile leadership roles, they have been conditioned to stand firm on their belief about how right they are. Otherwise, they worry that, in the eyes of others, being wrong will be construed as being weak. Leaders therefore have a natural tendency to defend their judgment at all costs.

Resilient leaders outgrow this tendency. As they strengthen their sense of self-efficacy, their confidence and competence to lead effectively, they grow into the realization that mistakes are just another way of learning. In fact, even though they may be quick to point out their mistakes, they realize that what really matters is what they learn from the mistakes. By reflecting on mistakes, leaders clarify what it takes to succeed in the future—the kind of skills, relationships, and approaches necessary for accomplishment.

A veteran high school principal confessed in an interview that he screwed up big time. In fact, he developed anxiety attacks from the anticipation of having to tell the faculty that he blew it when he mishandled confidential feedback he received from a teacher about another teacher's off duty conduct. The principal described his poor handling of the situation:

"A teacher, I'll call her Sue, asked to speak to me confidentially about a personal matter. She entered my office shut the door and said she was worried about a colleague in her department. She described an incident reported to her about her colleague saying to the class that he had a bad day and he wondered if any students would leave school, and get him some drugs so he could get through the day. A student quickly volunteered for the assignment, a student who had a reputation for dealing on the streets. Allegedly the teacher in question told the student to meet him in the hall, sneak out the back door and be back in school in time for next period."

The principal continued, "The student left, came back with a brown paper bag, and handed it to the teacher in exchange for some money. Sue said in the privacy of my office that the teacher had been acting rather flaky lately and she was worried about him doing drugs on the job. The whole thing spiraled out of control, because I confronted the student about the incident. The student told the teacher, who told other teachers about my accusations. The reality was this: the teacher walked into the hall with the student, instructed him to get some Tylenol PM for his migraine headaches that had been recurring, and the student complied. The student even produced the receipt from Walgreens."

"By the next day, the entire faculty was abuzz about my behavior, and let's face it, I blew it! I went home that night, went to the computer and created a business-sized card that read, "I blew it. I used poor judgment and you deserve better. This coupon is your guarantee that I won't make such a mistake again, and I will continue to earn your trust as a leader.

"I passed out the cards the next day at a faculty meeting. It was so hard to stand before them and say I screwed up. But admitting my error turned out to be positive in a lot of ways. The teachers made up 'I made a mistake' cards with similar language, and actually passed them out to students when the teachers messed up."

Less resilient leaders might have tried to hide behind excuses or blame others for things spiraling out of control. But as the previous example illustrated, owning up to errors in judgment lays the groundwork for an organizational culture that has integrity and is open to scrutiny in a transparent way. Things are not hidden and people are not blamed. Resilient leaders serve as a model when they acknowledge their own mistakes in judgment and accept account-ability for correcting their leadership conduct in the future.

In his book, *Good to Great,* Collins (2001) wrote, "In an era when leaders go to claim credit about how they were visionary when their colleagues were not, but finding others to blame when their decisions go awry, it is refreshing to find individuals who take responsibility for bad decisions" (p. 77). But bad decisions don't have to remain bad. They can be opportunities for knowledge and insight if leaders critically examine what happened, what they learned from it, and how they can use the experience to increase their capacity to confront future dilemmas.

Action Strategy: Resilient Leaders accept Responsibility for making needed changes Personally in those Cases where they Contributed to the Adversity

The previous strategy focused on admitting mistakes in judgment. This strategy begins with leaders realizing their conduct contributed to conditions that fueled the adversity. In other words, resilient leaders have the courage to step forward and say, "Because I did this (or didn't do this), I caused much of the mess we find ourselves in right now. And you have my assurance that I have learned from this. I will change my approach in the future to keep the mess from getting stirred up again."

In times of turmoil leaders sometimes feel like they have been involuntarily thrown from the frying pan directly into the fire. These situations require great strength and hardiness in leaders. Because they care, leaders frequently assume the role of caretaker for others, holding them together and meeting their emotional needs. The sense of responsibility can place great strain on the shoulders of leaders who feel compelled to protect those they serve.

In an effort to buffer staff from adversity looming close by, leaders hone the art of making truthful statements without fully disclosing more of the facts. This conduct can lead to a range of consequences, most of them unfavorable. For instance, a principal can fail to disclose to the teachers that the construction of the new high school likely will mean some teachers will be reassigned next year. When the truth, or full disclosure, finally comes out it is predictable that teachers will demand, "How long have you kept this from us?" With the best of intentions, the actions of the principal produced an attitude of mistrust at a time that tensions were already high regarding the impact of the new school. And the principal contributed to the mess by his actions.

In other circumstances, a leader's contribution to adversity is more at the personal level. The Wisconsin superintendent who faced the murder of a principal during the school day reflected, "The psychiatrist, who worked with us in the aftermath, was a wonderful resource. He called me every month, from January through June, each time asking, 'How are you doing?' My programmed response was 'I'm all right. Things are going fine.' In May I exploded at him, 'Why the hell are you calling me all the time?' He retorted, 'Because you are not fine. People in your position take care of others and deep six their own feelings and emotions.' Looking back, he was right. I wasn't doing fine. The gravity of the situation caused me to 'gunny sack' my emotions. Out of sight. Out of mind. Out of consideration."

By ignoring his own needs, the superintendent contributed to much of the fallout in his personal life. As he described it, he fell out of balance. While he was not responsible in any way for the act of violence by a deranged twenty-one year old, he did have a sense of guilt that maybe he could have done more to ensure security in the system. He needed an external resource to help him see clearly the situation and his role in it.

People forget that leadership is a very personal activity that is challenging cognitively, emotionally, physically, and spiritually. The weight of intense surroundings and circumstances in tandem with the pressure of time can obscure a leader's perspective. Sometimes leaders fool themselves that they are different from others in similar circumstances, and that they will not succumb to human frailties. The ego can kick into high gear, tricking them into thinking that they are shatterproof, indispensable and infallible.

Resilient leaders develop the wisdom to discern as objectively as possible their personal contributions to the issues. Their wisdom is strengthened through the application of several strategies.

First, they recognize and acknowledge their contribution to creating the pending problem. They examine past decisions and behavior and look first at what actions or inaction they took that helped create the furor. By doing so, they better understand the dynamics of the issue and consequences of their previous behavior.

Wise leaders consider several questions. First, what decisions or actions may have contributed to the problem? How many of my previous choices resulted in negative events? Now that I recognize the circumstances, what can I do to resolve them? Were my motivations to serve others, protect my ego, or preserve my image?

Second, resilient leaders own their own actions and don't fear being accountable. Acknowledging their contribution to creating the circumstances doesn't mean self-blame or sinking into depression. Basically it requires an affirmation that they could have responded in a more effective manner. They examine what they did or did *not* do to create the situation. They also analyze what other courses they may have taken and identify ways to reduce negative risk or impact on the state of affairs.

By applying these reflective strategies, as painful as they may be to contemplate, leaders become stronger and more able to respond effectively to future times of turmoil and stress.

SUMMARY

People rely on leaders in tragic times to demonstrate calm reassurance. But the decisions facing leaders are hard and wired with controversy. Sometimes these decisions alienate people—even supporters and friends. But for value-driven leaders that comes with the territory. Ethical principles are the drivers that lead to credibility and respect for the leader.

In turbulent times, resilient leaders do not duck personal responsibility. It is integral to their role and to their character. They stand tall, take the heat, and courageously accept their charge to provide credible leadership that will have a sustained, long-term impact on the success of the organization.

CHARTING YOUR RESILIENCE PROFILE FOR PERSONAL

To chart your Leader Resilience Profile for *Personal Responsibility,* return to your completed LRP Survey in Chapter 1, then follow these steps:

- For each item number listed, circle your *actual* item response on the chart.
- Determine the *conversion* score for the item, located directly beneath the *actual* number you circled.
- Enter your conversion score in the box on the extreme right column of the chart.
- Sum the scores in the right column to determine your Resilience Strength Score for *Personal Responsibility.*
- Observe your individualized score on the continuum from Moderately Low to Very High.

Table 10.1. Personal Responsibility Subscale

Strength: Personal Responsibility

Item #	Item Response	Enter your Conversion Score for the Item
6	If your *actual* item response is: 1 2 3 4 5 6 Then your *conversion* score is: 1 2 3 4 5 6 **enter your conversion score in the box →**	
12	If your *actual* item response is: 1 2 3 4 5 6 Then your *conversion* score is: 1 2 3 4 5 6 **enter your conversion score in the box →**	
18	If your *actual* item response is: 1 2 3 4 5 6 Then your *conversion* score is: 1 2 3 4 5 6 **enter your conversion score in the box →**	
25	If your *actual* item response is: 1 2 3 4 5 6 Then your *conversion* score is: 1 2 3 4 5 6 **enter your conversion score in the box →**	
62	If your *actual* item response is: 1 2 3 4 5 6 Then your *conversion* score is: 6 5 4 3 2 1 **enter your conversion score in the box →**	
67	If your *actual* item response is: 1 2 3 4 5 6 Then your *conversion* score is: 1 2 3 4 5 6 **enter your conversion score in the box →**	
	Strength Score: Personal Responsibility →	

Strength Score Continuum for Personal Responsibility

Resilience Level →	Moderately Low	Moderate	Moderately High	Very High
Score Range →	13–18	19–24	25–30	31–36

Part V

The Big Picture

OVERVIEW

In Part Five, we provide you a step-by-step, personalized Resilience Guide that you can implement right now.

The Resilience Guide begins in Chapter 11. We summarize the major concepts of leader resilience. Next we outline the nine resilience strengths discussed in the book and reflected in the Leader Resilience Profile ®. For each of the strengths, we pose reflective questions for you to contemplate as you seek ways to build resilience in this area. We close the chapter by referring you to the Leader Resilience Profile Chart, Appendix A, that lets you chart your "big picture" profile. You can determine your top strengths as well as those strengths that you feel deserve additional attention.

The next part of the Resilience Guide, Appendix B, contains 47 action strategies you can put into practice tomorrow. These action strategies directly map to the Leader Resilience Profile (LRP) statements. As you review your resilience areas of relative strength and areas for improvement, you can refer to *47 Action Strategies* for specific how-to ideas.

The final component of the Resilience Guide is our Web site, *www.theresilientleader.com*. On this site you will discover a wealth of information, tools, professional development activities, and related resources you can tap to strengthen your leader resilience and the resilience of your organization. The personalized Resilience Guide will be a tremendous asset as you answer the question, "Where do I go from here?" And, of course, feel free to contact Jerry Patterson or any member of the team directly at: *theresilientleader@ gmail.com*. We wish you a resilient future.

Chapter 11

Your Personalized Leader Resilience Guide

THE DEEPER MEANING OF RESILIENCE

We began *Resilient Leadership for Turbulent Times* with a discussion about what leader resilience is, as well as what it is not. Resilience is not a short-term concept. It is a long-term perspective about how leaders perceive and act on the inevitable adverse conditions they will confront in their leadership role. We define a resilient leader as a person who *demonstrates the ability to recover, learn from, and developmentally mature when confronted by chronic or crisis adversity.* We also discussed five phases of the resilience cycle, moving from normal conditions to deteriorating, adapting, recovering, and growing phases. For each phase we presented real-life examples of leaders as they struggled with adversity. At the close of Chapter 1 we invited you to complete the Leader Resilience Profile (LRP). The LRP is a comprehensive account of what comprises leader resilience. In subsequent chapters, we examined each of the nine resilience strengths and created a chart for you to assess your personal resilience for the strength discussed. Below we summarize the nine strengths.

RESILIENCE THINKING SKILLS

Resilience Strength #1: Optimism

Leader resilience starts here. As a well-worn bumper sticker reminds us, "It is not so much what you do. It's how you think about what you do that makes all the difference." Optimism consists of two components: how you think about current reality and how you think about the future.

The first step in the thinking process begins with how you think about reality. Resilient leaders want to understand, as comprehensively as possible, what is happening around them right now. They want to know the bad news and the good news. The second component of resilient thinking by leaders consists of how they envision future possibilities. They demonstrate the ability to maintain a positive outlook about the future when adversity strikes, but they don't deny the barriers posed by reality. Resilient leaders engage in reflective thinking to assess their relative optimism when they pose questions such as:

- How have I taken steps to understand reality from as many different perspectives as possible?
- In what ways have I worked hard to find the positive aspects of adversity to balance the negative aspects?
- What have I done to focus my energy on future opportunities, not the obstacles, when confronted by adversity?

As a reminder, you can convert all of the action strategies outlined in Appendix A to reflective questions. You can use these questions to provide a self-assessment of your resilience strength. And you can ask others you work with to offer their perspective in response to the questions.

CAPACITY BUILDING SKILLS

Adversity is virtually inevitable. How you choose to respond, however, is optional. We emphasized in Part Three of the book that the strength of your response to adversity depends, in large part, on your resilience capacity, the amount of energy you have available to act when storms strike. Even though your resilience capacity may seem low at the time adversity hits, your capacity is elastic over time. You expand your capacity as you successfully overcome adversity. This success gives you more resilience energy to tackle bigger problems in the future. Four leader resilience strengths comprise resilience capacity: personal values, personal efficacy, personal support base, and personal well-being.

Resilience Strength #2: Personal Values

In Chapter 5 we described a three-level hierarchy of values, beginning with ethical principles at the top, followed by the educational values that matter most to you, and then values you hold about specific program initiatives in your organization. We examined specific strategies that value-driven leaders use to build their resilience strength. You can gauge your relative strength in this area when you ask questions such as:

- To what extent have I privately clarified and public articulated my core values?
- In what ways have I taken leadership actions consistent with what matters most among competing values?
- What can I point to that demonstrates I make value-driven decisions in the face of strong opposition?

Resilience Strength #3: Personal Efficacy

We defined leader efficacy as the confidence plus the competence to exert consistent leadership when the going gets rough. Some leaders confess that they convey an artificial sense of efficacy. In one superintendent's words, "In my early years in this job my motto was, 'Fake it 'til you make it.' I call this bluff leadership. It works for a while, but authentic efficacy comes when I truly believe in my ability to lead, and then I act like it." You can get a sense of your efficacy when you honestly confront reflective questions like:

- In what ways have I attempted to offset any relative weakness in an area by turning to others who have strengths in the skills required?
- What can I identify that accurately reflects the level of knowledge and skills I possess to lead in tough times?
- Maintain a composed and respected leadership presence in the midst of adversity

Resilience Strength #4: Strong Support Base

The third energy source in your leadership fuel tank is your support base. We found that leaders who are resilient in the long run depend on trusted others to advise and listen to them in times of need. We did interview some leaders who felt they had to "go it alone" or their leadership would be construed as weak. However, the leaders who were resilient over the long haul knew their energy would eventually evaporate if they failed to call upon the strength of others to help them become personally stronger. We provided concrete examples of ways that friends, family, clergy, and colleagues stepped forward to offer support. You learn about the strength of your support base when you ponder questions such as:

- What have I learned from the experience of others who faced similar circumstances?
- To what extent have I been willing to make myself vulnerable to involve those I trust in a discussion about my doubts or fears?
- How have I actively sought to learn from role models who demonstrated a strong track record of resilience?

Resilience Strength #5: Personal Well-Being

In Chapter 6 we talked about the ESP of well-being: the emotional, spiritual, and physical dimensions of a leader's health, or well-being. We pointed out that these elements are interdependent on each other. For example a serious disease can take a toll on a leader's emotional health, too. Even though we consider ESP well-being to be organic, for discussion purposes we examined each element separately.

Emotional well-being consists of the ability to understand and effectively manage your emotions in times of adversity. Emotional well-being also refers to how you emotionally make sense of what is happening to you. The emotional interpretation of events can be dramatically changed by changing the emotional color of the lenses you use to view adversity. Resilient leaders adopt their own version of the Serenity Prayer, "Emotionally I accept things I cannot change, I change the things I can, and I have developed the wisdom to discern the difference." You contemplate your emotional health when you consider reflective questions like:

- How have I demonstrated my strength to emotionally accept those aspects of adversity that I can't influence in a positive way?
- To what extent do I truly understand my emotions in times of adversity and how these emotions affect my leadership performance?
- How successful have I been in gaining control of my emotions before I say or do something I would otherwise regret?

A second ingredient in personal health is a leader's spiritual well being. Some leaders we interviewed said that spirituality was not part of their belief system. Most, however, described a personalized interpretation of spirituality that consisted of two parts: a belief in a cause beyond one's self and a companion belief in a Universal source of strength greater than one's self. Sometimes the ultimate source was found in religion. In other instances, leaders talked about their belief in the power of a universal dynamic that serves the common good of humanity. In all cases, you can become more attuned to your spiritual self by asking:

- In what ways have I gained strength from my connection to a higher purpose in life?
- How have I expressed spiritual gratitude for the opportunity to pursue a calling to leadership?
- To what extent have I turned to personal reflection and introspection to steady myself during adversity?

Research in many fields produces inconclusive results. This is not the case in the area of physical health. A synthesis of research studies clearly documents that physical health directly affects a leader's overall sense of well-being. For most leaders, though, it seems so hard to align action with values. The constant struggle for leaders is how to find the *time* to make it happen. There are no shortcuts. To help stay on track in aligning your behavior with your professed values, reflect on questions like:

- How have I let adversity disrupt my long-term focus on a healthy lifestyle?
- What strategies have worked for me in managing my time devoted to rest and recovery?
- To what extent have I found healthy ways to channel my physical energy as a stress reliever?

Resilience Strength #6: Perseverance

Leaders demonstrate perseverance in the face of adversity when they voluntarily and relentlessly pursue a course of action, consistent with their core values about what matters most, and without regard for discouragement, barriers or previous failure. They don't give up! And they are rewarded on the other side of adversity with a renewed sense of efficacy because they have proven to themselves that they have the confidence and competence to survive, even thrive, in the face of tough times. You can take stock of your own perseverance strength by asking reflective questions like:

- In what instances have I remained persistent through tough times until I succeeded in achieving my goal?
- To what extent have I avoided letting disruptive forces interfere with my focus on important goals?
- How have I been able to keep adversity in one aspect of my life from having a long-term impact on other parts of my life?

Resilience Strength #7: Adaptability

Chapter 8 began with the question, "What is adaptive leadership and how do you know it when you see it?" We discussed the risk leaders take when they act "against the grain" by making mid-course adjustments in their leadership approach. Then we examined specific steps leaders can take to become more adaptable in light of constantly shifting sand of change. The following questions will help you take stock of how you have already have implemented some of these steps:

- In what ways have I adjusted my strategies as the circumstances surrounding adversity changed?
- To what extent have I shown the ability to put my mistakes in perspective and move beyond them?
- How have I used feedback about the reality of what's happening to modify my leadership strategies?

Resilience Strength #8: Courageous Decision-Making

Virtually all leaders arrive at their first leadership jobs with a track record of demonstrating courage. Whether implicit or explicitly stated, courage is a prerequisite to successful leadership. As one leader observed, "Any leader can demonstrate courage to do the right things when things are going right. It becomes involved much greater risk to take leadership actions in the heat of the battle." In Chapter 9, we illustrated how leaders can demonstrate this courage during crisis conditions, and we provided examples where leaders told us about how they found the courage to act in concert with their convictions. You can provide your own examples by reflecting on these questions:

- To what extent have I taken appropriate leadership actions, even when some things were still ambiguous or confusing?
- What is my track record for taking prompt, decisive action in emergency situations demanding an immediate response?
- How have I demonstrated the ability to make principled decisions that, at times, were contrary to advice or pressure by others?

Resilience Strength #9: Personal Responsibility

The term *responsibilities* appears in most leaders' job descriptions so, at first glance, it may seem unnecessary to devote an entire chapter to leader duties. However, if we probe beneath the surface we discover many secrets that experienced leaders already know but didn't learn in their administrator preparation programs. Our purpose in Chapter 10 was to highlight the multiple facets of personal responsibility, including moral responsibility, accountability for results, and responsibility to serve as steward for the common good of the community or, as one leader said, "The keeper of the keys that unlocks student learning." These responsibilities take on added weight when leaders face crisis and chronic adversity. This burden becomes more conspicuous when leaders move off the dance floor to the balcony and reflect on how they have conducted themselves under fire. We have listed reflective questions below that we ask you to consider:

- To what extent have I accepted accountability for the long-term organizational impact of any tough leadership decisions I made?
- In what instances have I taken responsibility to make hard choices that may negatively impact some individuals or groups?
- How extensively have I assumed responsibility to make needed changes personally in those cases where I contributed to the adversity?

THE BIG PICTURE: YOUR PERSONALIZED LEADER RESILIENCE PROFILE

The remaining parts of your personalized Leader Resilience Guide are found in Appendix A and Appendix B. We began the book with the big picture concepts of resilience, including a description of the resilience cycle that all leaders follow en route to recovering, learning from, and developmentally maturing after the shock of serious adversity. We devoted nine chapters to a careful examination of the nine strengths of resilient leaders. Now it is time to look at the big picture again, this time in the form of your overall Leader Resilience Profile. In Appendix B, you will find the nine strengths, and some associated subcategories for Optimism and Personal Well-Being. Take a few moments to locate your resilience strength score that you charted in previous chapters and transfer the data to your individualized profile in Appendix A. This provides you a snapshot of the patterns you developed through the book.

Returning to a question we raised earlier, "Where do I go from here?", you now have a way of identifying the strengths that stand out in both directions, excellence and improvement. You can develop an action plan for becoming more resilient than ever by using the Leader Resilience Checklist in Appendix B. The checklist refers you once again to concrete strategies that you can put in place tomorrow to accelerate your pace in the journey from surviving to thriving as a resilient leader. We hope we have contributed to your resilience and we wish you safe travel in your journey.

Appendix A

Personalized Leader Resilience Profile

Leader Resilience Profile

Strength Category	*Resilience Strength Score Continuum*				
	Thinking Skills				
Understanding Reality:	6 7 8 9 10 11 Low	12 13 14 15 16 17 Moderately Low	18 19 20 21 22 23 Moderate	24 25 26 27 28 29 Moderately High	30 31 32 33 34 35 36 Very High
Envisioning the Future:	6 7 8 9 10 11 Low	12 13 14 15 16 17 Moderately Low	18 19 20 21 22 23 Moderate	24 25 26 27 28 29 Moderately High	30 31 32 33 34 35 36 Very High
	Capacity Skills				
Personal Values:	6 7 8 9 10 11 Low	12 13 14 15 16 17 Moderately Low	18 19 20 21 22 23 Moderate	24 25 26 27 28 29 Moderately High	30 31 32 33 34 35 36 Very High
Personal Efficacy:	6 7 8 9 10 11 Low	12 13 14 15 16 17 Moderately Low	18 19 20 21 22 23 Moderate	24 25 26 27 28 29 Moderately High	30 31 32 33 34 35 36 Very High
Personal Support Base:	6 7 8 9 10 11 Low	12 13 14 15 16 17 Moderately Low	18 19 20 21 22 23 Moderate	24 25 26 27 28 29 Moderately High	30 31 32 33 34 35 36 Very High
Emotional Well-Being:	6 7 8 9 10 11 Low	12 13 14 15 16 17 Moderately Low	18 19 20 21 22 23 Moderate	24 25 26 27 28 29 Moderately High	30 31 32 33 34 35 36 Very High
Spiritual Well-Being:	6 7 8 9 10 11 Low	12 13 14 15 16 17 Moderately Low	18 19 20 21 22 23 Moderate	24 25 26 27 28 29 Moderately High	30 31 32 33 34 35 36 Very High
Physical Well-Being:	6 7 8 9 10 11 Low	12 13 14 15 16 17 Moderately Low	18 19 20 21 22 23 Moderate	24 25 26 27 28 29 Moderately High	30 31 32 33 34 35 36 Very High
	Action Skills				
Perseverance:	6 7 8 9 10 11 Low	12 13 14 15 16 17 Moderately Low	18 19 20 21 22 23 Moderate	24 25 26 27 28 29 Moderately High	30 31 32 33 34 35 36 Very High
Adaptability:	6 7 8 9 10 11 Low	12 13 14 15 16 17 Moderately Low	18 19 20 21 22 23 Moderate	24 25 26 27 28 29 Moderately High	30 31 32 33 34 35 36 Very High
Courageous Decision Making:	6 7 8 9 10 11 Low	12 13 14 15 16 17 Moderately Low	18 19 20 21 22 23 Moderate	24 25 26 27 28 29 Moderately High	30 31 32 33 34 35 36 Very High
Personal Responsibility:	6 7 8 9 10 11 Low	12 13 14 15 16 17 Moderately Low	18 19 20 21 22 23 Moderate	24 25 26 27 28 29 Moderately High	30 31 32 33 34 35 36 Very High

Appendix B

Resilient Leadership Checklist

STRENGTH: OPTIMISM

Resilient leaders:

- Come to terms with the reality that adversity likely will show up unexpectedly and disrupt their best laid plans.
- Pay attention to the reality of any external forces that could limit what they would like to accomplish ideally.
- Search for the positive aspects of adversity to balance the negative aspects.
- Find ways to have a positive influence in making good things happen.
- Expect good things will come out of an adverse situation.
- Focus their energy on the opportunities, not the obstacles, found in a bad situation.
- Maintain a respectful sense of humor in the face of adverse circumstances.

STRENGTH: VALUE-DRIVEN

Resilient leaders:

- Privately clarify and publicly articulate their core values.
- Rely *foremost* on strongly held moral or ethical principles to guide them through adversity.
- Act on what matters most to them among competing values.
- Consistently gather feedback to make sure they are walking their talk.
- Make value-driven decisions even in the face of strong opposition.

STRENGTH: PERSONAL EFFICACY

Resilient leaders:

- Try to offset any relative leadership weakness they have in an area by turning to others who have strength in this area.
- Remain confident that they can learn from their adversity to help them be stronger in the future.
- Maintain a confident presence as leader in the midst of adversity.
- Take a deliberate, step-by-step approach to overcome adversity.
- Demonstrate the essential knowledge and skills to lead in tough times.

STRENGTH: SUPPORT BASE

Resilient leaders:

- Learn from the professional experiences of others who faced similar circumstances.
- Have the resources of a strong personal support base to help them through tough times in their leadership role.
- Never hesitate to tell those they trust about their doubts or fears related to adversity.
- Feel comfortable sharing with their support base any small wins they achieve along the road to recovering from adversity.

STRENGTH: PERSONAL WELL-BEING

Resilient leaders:

- Emotionally accept those things they cannot influence in a positive way.
- Emotionally let go of any goal they are pursuing if it's causing them to sacrifice more important long-term goals and values.
- Stay in touch with their emotions during adversity and realize how their emotions affect their leadership performance.
- Turn to personal reflection or connections to a higher purpose in life as a source of strength during adversity.
- Feel a deep spiritual gratitude for the opportunity to pursue a calling of leadership, especially during tough times.
- Protect time to renew their emotional, physical, and spiritual well-being.

STRENGTH: PERSEVERANCE

Resilient leaders:

- Never let disruptive forces and other distractions interfere with the leadership focus on important goals and tasks.
- Become more persevering than ever when confronted with the next round of adversity.
- Maintain a steady, concentrated focus on the most important priorities until success is attained.
- Strive to keep adversity in one aspect of their life from having a long-term impact on resilience in other parts of their life.
- Persistently refuse to give up, unless it is *absolutely clear* that all realistic strategies have been exhausted.

STRENGTH: ADAPTABILITY

Resilient leaders:

- Use ongoing feedback about the reality of what's happening and possible in the future and make adjustments in leadership strategies.
- Adjust expectations about what is possible based on what is learned about the reality of the current situation.
- Demonstrate the ability to put mistakes in perspective and move beyond them.
- Search for workable strategies to achieve positive results in difficult situations.
- Quickly change course, as needed, to adapt to rapidly changing circumstances.

STRENGTH: COURAGEOUS DECISION-MAKING

Resilient leaders:

- Take appropriate action, even when some things about the situation are ambiguous or confusing.
- Take prompt, principled action on unexpected threats before they escalate out of control.
- Make principled decisions that, at times, are contrary to respected advice by others.

- Take prompt, decisive action in emergency situations demanding an immediate response.
- Seek perspectives that differ significantly from their own, so they can make the most informed decisions possible under tough conditions.

STRENGTH: PERSONAL RESPONSIBILITY

Resilient leaders:

- Accept responsibility for making tough choices that may negatively affect some individuals or groups.
- Are always aware that when they decide not to take action in the face of adversity, they have to assume personal responsibility for that action.
- Accept accountability for the long-term organizational impact of any tough leadership decision they make.
- Acknowledge mistakes in judgment and assume responsibility for making the necessary changes in the future.
- Accept responsibility for making needed changes personally in those cases where they contributed to the adversity.

References

Badaracco, J. L., Jr. (1997). *Defining moments: When managers must choose between right and right.* Boston: Harvard Business School Press.

Bennis, W. G., & Thomas, R. J. (2002). *Geeks & geezers: How era, values, and defining moments shape leaders.* Boston: Harvard Business School Press.

Bolman, L. G. & Deal, T. E. (2008). *Reframing organizations: Artistry, choice and leadership.* San Francisco: Jossey-Bass.

Burns, J. M. (1978). *Leadership.* New York: Harper & Row.

Cameron, K. S., Dutton, J. E., & Quinn, R. E. (2003). Foundations of Positive Organizational Scholarship. In Cameron, K. S., Dutton, J. E., & Quinn, R. E. (Eds.), *Positive organizational scholarship: Foundations of a new discipline* (pp. 3–13). San Francisco: Berrett-Koehler Publishers, Inc.

Carver, C. S. & Scheier, M. F. (2003). Three human strengths. In L. G. Aspinwall & U. M. Staudinger (Eds.), *A psychology of human strengths: Fundamental questions and future directions for a positive psychology* (pp. 87–102). San Francisco: Berrett-Koehler Publishers Inc.

Collins, J. C. (2001). *Good to great: Why some companies make the leap—and others don't.* New York: Harper Business.

Cottrell, D. (2007). *Monday morning leadership: 8 mentoring sessions you can't afford to miss.* Dallas, TX: CornerStone Leadership.

Csikszentmihalyi, M. (1990). *Flow: The psychology of optimal experience.* New York: Harper & Row.

Davidson, J. & Dreher, H. (2003). *The anxiety book: Developing strength in the face of fear.* New York: Riverhead Books.

Emmons, R. (2007). *Thanks! How the new science of gratitude can make you happier.* Boston: Houghton Mifflin Company.

Fullan, M. (2001). *The new meaning of educational change* (3rd ed.). New York: Teachers College Press.

Goens, G. A. (2005). *Soft leadership for hard times.* Lanham, Md: Rowman & Littlefield Education.

Goleman, D. (1995). *Emotional intelligence.* New York: Bantam Books.

Heifetz, R. A. (1994). *Leadership without easy answers.* Cambridge, Mass: Belknap Press of Harvard University Press.

Houston, P. D., Blankstein, A. M., & Cole, R. W. (Eds.). (2008). *Spirituality in educational leadership.* Thousand Oaks, CA: Corwin Press.

Houston, P. D. & Sokolow, S. L. (2006). *The spiritual dimension of leadership: 8 key principles to leading more effectively.* Thousands Oaks, CA: Corwin Press.

Jazzar, M. & Kimball, D. P. (2004). Lonely at the top. *The New Superintendent Journal, 61,*(2), 42–44.

Kolditz, T. A. (2007) In extremis leadership. San Francisco: Jossey-Bass.

Luthans, F. (2002). Positive organizational behavior: Developing and managing psychological strengths for performance improvement. *Academy of Management Executive, 16,* 57–75.

Mayer, J. D., Salovey, P. & Caruso, D. (2000). Models of emotional intelligence. In R. J. Sternberg (Ed.). *The handbook of intelligence* (pp. 396–420). New York: Cambridge University Press.

Moyer, D. (2009). Is experience enough? [Special issue]. *Harvard Business Review, 120*(1).

Pascale, R. T., Milleman, M. & Gioja, L. (2000). *Surfing the edge of chaos.* New York: Three Rivers Press.

Patterson, J. (2000). *The anguish of leadership.* Arlington, VA: American Association of School Administrators.

Patterson, J. L. & Kelleher, P. (2005). *Resilient school leaders: Strategies for turning adversity into achievement.* Alexandria. Virginia: Association for Supervision and Curriculum Development

Patterson, J. L., Goens, G. A., & Reed, D. E. (2008). Joy & resilience: Strange bedfellows. *School Administrator. 65*(11), 28–29.

Patterson, J., Patterson, J., Reed, D. & Riddle, L. (2008). *Leadership resilience profile: A technical supplement.* Unpublished manuscript. University of Alabama-Birmingham.

Pearsall, P. (2003). *The Beethoven factor: The new positive psychology hardiness, happiness, healing and hope.* Charlottesville, VA: Hampton Roads Publishing Company, Inc.

Peterson, C., & Seligman, M. E. P. (2004). *Character strengths and virtues: A handbook and classification.* Washington, DC: American Psychological Association.

Reivich, K., & Shatte, A. (2002). The resilience factor: 7 essential skills for overcoming life's inevitable obstacles. New York: Broadway Books.

Schilling, E. F. (2008). Use emotional intelligence to improve your work. *Women in Higher Education, 17*(6), 19–20.

Schulman, P. (1999). Applying learned optimism to increase sales productivity. *Journal of Personal Selling and Sales Management, 19,* 31–37.

Seligman, M. E. P. (1991). *Learned optimism.* New York: Knopf.

Stone, F. M. (2007). *Coaching, counseling & mentoring: How to choose & reuse the right technique to boost employee performance* (2nd ed.). New York: American Management Association.

Tice, D. M., & Baumeister, R. F. (1997). Longitudinal study of procrastination, performance, stress, and health: The costs and benefits of dawdling. *Psychological Science, 8*(6), 454–458.

Tichy, N. M., & Bennis, W. G. (2007). *Judgment: How winning leaders make great calls.* New York: Portfolio.

Tolle, E. (2005). *A new earth: Awakening to your life's purpose.* New York: Penguin Group.

Wheatley, M. J. (2005). *Finding our way: Leadership for an uncertain time.* San Francisco: Berrett-Koehler.

Wheatley, M. J., & Kellner-Rogers, M. (1996). *A simpler way.* San Francisco: Berrett-Koehler.

Wheatley, M. (1999). *Leadership and the new science.* San Francisco: Barrett-Koehler Publishers.

Whyte, D. (2001). *Crossing the unknown sea: Work as a pilgrimage of identity.* New York: Riverhead Books.

About the Authors

Jerry Patterson is the nation's leading authority on leadership resilience. With more than 200,000 copies of his books in print, he is the author of ten nationally recognized books on leadership and resilience, as well as numerous articles in leading professional journals. Patterson currently is Professor of Leadership Studies at the University of Alabama at Birmingham. In his more than 30 years of experience as an educator, he has served as a superintendent, assistant superintendent, curriculum director, elementary school principal, and high school teacher.

In addition to leading, teaching, and writing, Patterson has conducted workshops and presentations to over 20,000 educators and other leaders in the United States, and internationally he has trained educational leaders in Slovakia, Israel, Nepal, Ecuador, Spain, and Canada. Patterson's focus is in the areas of leader resilience, leadership development, and culture change. Patterson can be reached at the School of Education, University of Alabama at Birmingham, USA, by phone at 205-975-5946 or e-mail at jpat@uab.edu.

George A. Goens has worked as a consultant with public and private sector organizations on leadership selection, development, and assessment. He has written three books and has published over 55 articles in professional journals and the mass media on leadership, change, and education. His latest two books were published by Allyn and Bacon and Rowman and Littlefield. He also served as a superintendent of schools. Email: gagoens@snet.net

Diane Reed is an Associate Professor and Co-Director of the Graduate Leadership Department at St. John Fisher College in Rochester, New York. Reed has been a school superintendent, assistant superintendent, elementary school principal, middle school English teacher, and elementary teacher. She is a member of the Governing Board of the American Association of School Administrators (AASA), Past Chair of the New York State Association of Women in Administration (NYSAWA), and past president-elect of the New York State Council of School Superintendents (NYSCOSS). E-mail:dreed@ sjfc.edu